OUYA Game Development by Example Beginner's Guide

An all-inclusive, fun guide to making professional 3D games for the OUYA console

Jack Donovan

PUBLISHING

BIRMINGHAM - MUMBAI

OUYA Game Development by Example Beginner's Guide

First published: May 2014

Production Reference: 1130514

Published by Packt Publishing Ltd.
Livery Place
35 Livery Street
Birmingham B3 2PB, UK.

ISBN 978-1-84969-722-4

www.packtpub.com

Cover Image by Suresh Mogre (suresh.mogre.99@gmail.com)

Credits

Author

Jack Donovan

Reviewers

Corey Blackburn

John P. Doran

Adam Sheehan

Commissioning Editor

Erol Staveley

Acquisition Editor

James Jones

Content Development Editor

Vaibhav Pawar

Technical Editors

Ritika Singh

Rohit Kumar Singh

Copy Editors

Sayanee Mukherjee

Deepa Nambiar

Karuna Narayanan

Laxmi Subramanian

Project Coordinator

Kranti Berde

Proofreaders

Ameesha Green

Paul Hindle

Indexers

Monica Ajmera Mehta

Priya Subramani

Graphics

Abhinash Sahu

Production Coordinator

Nilesh R. Mohite

Cover Work

Nilesh R. Mohite

About the Author

Jack Donovan is a game developer and a co-founder of Team Aurora Games, an independent game studio located in Burlington, Vermont. He founded Team Aurora Games with a group of his college peers because they wanted an outlet for creative projects that could eventually evolve into fully marketable games. He has been coding games in the Unity game engine since 2010, and has been working with the OUYA console ever since the initial developer kit release in 2012.

He programs primarily in C#, C++, Objective-C, and JavaScript. He has extensive experience in the DirectX, XNA, and Unity libraries and has developed his own homemade engines as well.

He is also a passionate technical writer. He has contributed DIY/instructional articles to Wired.com and Popular Science magazine, covering several unique hardware and software projects.

He studied at Champlain College, which he graduated from in May 2014 with a Bachelor of Science degree in Game Programming.

When he's not making games, he loves playing them with friends and discovering new ideas and concepts. He's an avid music listener and coffee drinker, both of which helped make this book possible.

He can be reached at jack@teamauroragames.com, and all of his present and future projects can be found at teamauroragames.com.

Acknowledgments

I'd like to thank everyone at Packt Publishing who played a role in the creation of this book, including my Project Coordinator, Kranti Berde, and Content Development Editor, Vaibhav Pawar. Writing this book has been a remarkable experience for me, and it wouldn't have been possible without their guidance and organization.

I'd also like to thank my colleagues at Team Aurora Games, who continue to be a great inspiration to keep growing and making games that I love.

Finally, an immense thanks to my family, friends, and mentors who supported me throughout the entire project and offered the wisdom and motivation that drove this book.

About the Reviewers

Corey Blackburn has always enjoyed video games since he was a child. During high school, he attended DigiPen Video Game Programming and Animation, an outreach program at Sea-Tac Occupational Skills Center. It was here that he developed a passion for programming. Since then, Corey continued on with his passion for game development and attended DigiPen Institute of Technology where he earned a Bachelor of Science degree in Computer Science in Real-time Interactive Simulation. During his senior year, Corey also worked part-time for 2clams studios, inc. developing a mobile game for Android and iOS, called *Housewife Wars*. Corey has also attended a McCarthy Bootcamp, where he learned The Core Protocols and has adapted them into his life. He has a passion for team building and enjoys working with tight-knit teams with a shared vision to make great games.

Corey is currently working as an indie developer for two Seattle-based start-ups, ACE Teams Co. that is developing *Spirit Siege* and Black Howler Studios that is working on *Iron Star*.

> I would like to thank my parents for all their support for turning my passion for playing video games into a career in game development.

John P. Doran is a technical game designer who has been creating games for over 10 years. He has worked on an assortment of games in teams from just himself to over 70 in student, mod, and professional projects.

He previously worked at LucasArts on *Star Wars: 1313* as a game design intern. He later graduated from DigiPen Institute of Technology in Redmond, WA, with a Bachelor of Science degree in Game Design.

John is currently working at DigiPen's Singapore campus as the lead instructor of DigiPen-Ubisoft Campus Game Programming Program, instructing graduate-level students in an intensive, advanced-level game programming curriculum. In addition to that, he also tutors and assists students on various subjects while giving lectures on C++, Unreal, Flash, Unity, and other such subjects.

He is the author of *Getting Started with UDK*, *Mastering UDK Game Development*, and he co-authored *UDK iOS Game Development Beginner's Guide*, all available from *Packt Publishing*.

Adam Sheehan first started programming at the age of 13, creating clones of retro video games in C and C++. Since then, he's dabbled in various forms of application and web development working with C#, Java, and Ruby. He currently spends his days teaching aspiring web developers Ruby on Rails at Launch Academy in Boston, MA.

www.PacktPub.com

Support files, eBooks, discount offers, and more

You might want to visit www.PacktPub.com for support files and downloads related to your book.

Did you know that Packt offers eBook versions of every book published, with PDF and ePub files available? You can upgrade to the eBook version at www.PacktPub.com and as a print book customer, you are entitled to a discount on the eBook copy. Get in touch with us at service@packtpub.com for more details.

At www.PacktPub.com, you can also read a collection of free technical articles, sign up for a range of free newsletters and receive exclusive discounts and offers on Packt books and eBooks.

http://PacktLib.PacktPub.com

Do you need instant solutions to your IT questions? PacktLib is Packt's online digital book library. Here, you can access, read and search across Packt's entire library of books.

Why subscribe?

- ◆ Fully searchable across every book published by Packt
- ◆ Copy and paste, print and bookmark content
- ◆ On demand and accessible via web browser

Free access for Packt account holders

If you have an account with Packt at www.PacktPub.com, you can use this to access PacktLib today and view nine entirely free books. Simply use your login credentials for immediate access.

Table of Contents

Preface

Independent video games are larger than ever, and are finally easy to create for anyone passionate about gaming. Over the past few years, the technology to create games has been made easier and more available. There are now free, beginner-friendly engines, such as Unity3D, which novice coders can use to create functioning prototypes in a matter of hours. With the release of the OUYA console, an Android-based console created as a publishing platform exclusively for independent developers, indie games can now be published and played on any TV in the comfort of your living room, making indie games even more pervasive and profitable. This book will give you everything you need to get started with creating three-dimensional games for OUYA as fast as possible, and provide you with the knowledge you'll need to keep growing as an indie developer by the time you reach the end of the book.

What this book covers

Chapter 1, Experiencing the OUYA, demonstrates the usage of the OUYA console and examines its user interface and technological capabilities.

Chapter 2, Installing Unity and the OUYA ODK, shows you how to install and configure the development environment required to create games for OUYA using the Unity3D game engine.

Chapter 3, Diving into Development, describes the anatomy of a basic script in the Unity3D engine and shows you how to create your first basic prototype.

Chapter 4, Moving Your Player with Controller Input, discusses how to create an interactive player object that responds to input from the OUYA controller.

Chapter 5, Enhancing Your Game with Touch Dynamics, talks about the built-in uses of the OUYA controller touchpad in the Unity3D engine and extends its functionality to create custom touch gesture mechanics.

Chapter 6, Saving Data to Create Longer Games, implements a basic data saving and loading functionality in prototypes from previous chapters and helps you understand the value of saving progress and other information.

Chapter 7, Expanding Your Gameplay with In-app Purchases, ensures that your prototypes meet the OUYA content guidelines required to sell a game on the OUYA marketplace. It also explains the finer aspects of packaging and polishing a game in Unity, including visual improvements, menus, and tutorials.

Chapter 8, Polishing and Prepping Your Game for Deployment, illustrates how to create both kinds of in-app purchases supported by the OUYA SDK and explains the differences between the purchases and the applications of each.

Chapter 9, Blazing Your Own Development Trail, helps establish the knowledge you need to grow as a game developer on your own and explores several techniques and tricks not covered in previous chapters.

What you need for this book

To use this book, you'll need a PC that is running a Mac OS X or a Windows operating system as well as an OUYA console to test and play your games on, including all related hardware (a USB cable, controller, display cable, and so on). You'll also need to install the Unity3D engine, which is available for download at http://www.unity3d.com/.

Who this book is for

This book is for anyone who wants to become an independent video game developer but doesn't know where to start. The OUYA console and Unity3D game development engine were both made with small-scale development and ease-of-use in mind, so you'll use both of these to prototype several different games and mechanics and learn how to make your dream games come to life.

Conventions

In this book, you will find several headings appearing frequently.

To give clear instructions of how to complete a procedure or task, we use:

Time for action – heading

1. Action 1
2. Action 2
3. Action 3

Instructions often need some extra explanation so that they make sense, so they are followed with:

What just happened?

This heading explains the working of tasks or instructions that you have just completed.

You will also find some other learning aids in the book, including:

Pop quiz – heading

These are short multiple-choice questions intended to help you test your own understanding.

Have a go hero – heading

These practical challenges give you ideas for experimenting with what you have learned.

You will also find a number of styles of text that distinguish between different kinds of information. Here are some examples of these styles, and an explanation of their meaning.

Code words in text, database table names, folder names, filenames, file extensions, pathnames, dummy URLs, user input, and Twitter handles are shown as follows: "Open your `RollingMarble` Unity project and double-click on the scene that has your level in it."

A block of code is set as follows:

```
void Update()
{
  if(Input.GetKeyDown(KeyCode.Return))
  {
    print(ChangeColor(Color.green));
  }
  else if(Input.GetKeyDown(KeyCode.Space))
  {
    print(ChangeColor(Color.blue));
  }
}
```

Any command-line input or output is written as follows:

```
source ~/.bash_profile
```

New terms and **important words** are shown in bold. Words that you see on the screen, in menus or dialog boxes for example, appear in the text like this: "Click on **Sign up** on the following page and follow the instructions to create your OUYA developer account."

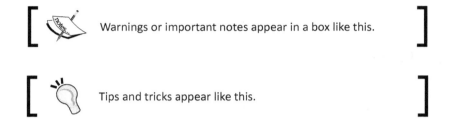

Warnings or important notes appear in a box like this.

Tips and tricks appear like this.

Reader feedback

Feedback from our readers is always welcome. Let us know what you think about this book— what you liked or may have disliked. Reader feedback is important for us to develop titles that you really get the most out of.

To send us general feedback, simply send an e-mail to feedback@packtpub.com, and mention the book title through the subject of your message.

If there is a topic that you have expertise in and you are interested in either writing or contributing to a book, see our author guide on www.packtpub.com/authors.

Customer support

Now that you are the proud owner of a Packt book, we have a number of things to help you to get the most from your purchase.

Downloading the example code

You can download the example code files for all Packt books you have purchased from your account at http://www.packtpub.com. If you purchased this book elsewhere, you can visit http://www.packtpub.com/support and register to have the files e-mailed directly to you.

Downloading the color images of this book

We also provide you a PDF file that has color images of the screenshots used in this book. You can download this file from `http://www.packtpub.com/sites/default/files/downloads/7224OT_ColorGraphics.pdf`.

Errata

Although we have taken every care to ensure the accuracy of our content, mistakes do happen. If you find a mistake in one of our books—maybe a mistake in the text or the code—we would be grateful if you would report this to us. By doing so, you can save other readers from frustration and help us improve subsequent versions of this book. If you find any errata, please report them by visiting `http://www.packtpub.com/submit-errata`, selecting your book, clicking on the **errata submission form** link, and entering the details of your errata. Once your errata are verified, your submission will be accepted and the errata will be uploaded to our website, or added to any list of existing errata, under the Errata section of that title.

Piracy

Piracy of copyright material on the Internet is an ongoing problem across all media. At Packt, we take the protection of our copyright and licenses very seriously. If you come across any illegal copies of our works, in any form, on the Internet, please provide us with the location address or website name immediately so that we can pursue a remedy.

Please contact us at `copyright@packtpub.com` with a link to the suspected pirated material.

We appreciate your help in protecting our authors, and our ability to bring you valuable content.

Questions

You can contact us at `questions@packtpub.com` if you are having a problem with any aspect of the book, and we will do our best to address it.

1
Experiencing the OUYA

The OUYA is a powerful and unique machine, because it gives hobbyists and independent developers a way to create and deploy professional-grade games without an overwhelming amount of groundwork. To begin making games for the OUYA, you won't need more than a basic understanding of game mechanics and a passion for development. This book will take you from your first prototype to a polished product ready to make its debut in the OUYA marketplace.

The lessons in this book will be demonstrated using the Unity3D engine, a popular development engine that's simple to learn with essential systems such as physics and user interface already built in. Unity and the OUYA both support a variety of scripting languages, but in this book, we'll be focusing on C#, a relatively easy yet versatile language that supports virtually any data structure your game will need.

You may already be familiar with the Unity engine; several popular games, such as *Temple Run 2* by Imangi Studios and *Scrolls* by Mojang (of *Minecraft* fame), have been built using Unity. You'll soon learn that the OUYA can take full advantage of the 3D capabilities of Unity to make the game of your dreams become real.

This first chapter will be a basic review of the default configuration of the OUYA and a demonstration of its capabilities using a game as an example. If you've already had some time to play around with your OUYA and you feel ready to get started with development, feel free to skip ahead to the next chapter, where we'll install our development environment and start deploying code to the console.

Setting up the console

Before diving in, you'll have to set your console up. If you've already plugged it in and taken it for a spin, it's still a good idea to check for system updates and make sure your video settings are optimal.

Networking

Once you've plugged your OUYA in and started it up for the first time, it will ask you to configure Internet settings, either wirelessly or with an Ethernet cable. This is an important step because a network connection allows us to view the latest games submitted to the marketplace, and we'll also be able to download the latest version of the OUYA software for development. Once you've completed the configuration, you'll reach the launch screen, which looks similar to the following screenshot:

Displaying games

The OUYA console and the Unity engine are both able to display games in 1080p HD, so it's best to develop them on a monitor that supports widescreen. It's also good to make sure that the OUYA display fits within the bounds of your monitor, because you need an accurate reference when developing your user interface to make sure it doesn't run off the screen (we'll get more into this in the later chapters). The following are a few ways to do this:

- Set your monitor's display ratio to **1:1** or **Just Scan**
- Check your monitor for a **Display Area** setting and adjust it to fit the screen
- Enable **Overscan compensation** in the **Advanced** settings in the HDMI menu

Time for action – installing your first game

Perform the following steps to install your first game in OUYA:

1. Now that you've covered the technical details, you can download a game from the OUYA marketplace to experience what a popular OUYA game looks like, and note small details that you can start thinking about for your own games. We'll use Canabalt HD as an example game, the latest iteration of Adam Saltsman's 2009 endless runner.

2. Click on the **Discover** button on the OUYA launch screen and you'll be brought to the marketplace's storefront, a showcase of featured games organized into several categories. This is where you'll see your published games once they gain some popularity. The following screenshot shows the storefront:

3. Press the Y button on your OUYA controller to bring up the search menu. Using the onscreen keyboard, search for Canabalt HD and then select it in the list of results. You'll be taken to the store page for Canabalt; here, you can click on **DOWNLOAD** and begin installing it on your console. The store page looks as shown in the following screenshot:

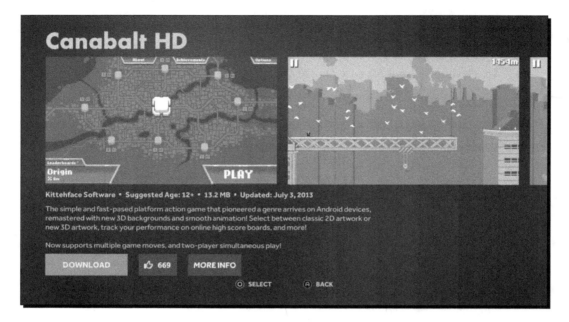

The **DOWNLOAD** button will turn into a **PLAY NOW** button once the installation process is complete. You can start the game directly from here or from the **PLAY** menu on the OUYA launch screen.

What just happened?

You've just successfully downloaded your first game on your OUYA console. The marketplace can be used to find all sorts of games that are always free to try, and once you download them, you can play them anytime from the OUYA's **PLAY** menu.

You may be wondering why you didn't see any prices while browsing the OUYA store or even while downloading your first title. Does this mean that all games for the OUYA are free to download? Well, the short answer is yes, but it's a little more complicated than that. Instead of following a conventional pricing system, the OUYA marketplace does things a little differently by providing at least one free element in each game. Canabalt incorporates monetization in the form of free-play credits, shown in the following screenshot:

In the case of Canabalt HD, the developers decided to offer a trial version that includes five free plays per day and an option to pay for an upgrade that unlocks unlimited play. The player can also unlock additional plays by making it past the 5000-meter mark in the game. However, this isn't the only payment model you can use; as long as there's something free in your game, you can have as many or as few purchasing options as you want. For instance, you could create a game that features unlimited playtime but limited free items, or make a game that's free up until a certain level. The OUYA SDK has an in-app purchase API that will let you get creative with priced elements in your game.

Playing the OUYA

Now that the technical stuff is out of the way, take a few minutes (or several) to play Canabalt and get a feel of how the OUYA performs. Despite being part of the console family, the OUYA varies from its siblings such as the PS3 and Xbox 360. The games are often smaller and less expensive than full triple-A titles because of the abundant indie presence. You'll notice a few features about Canabalt that are pretty typical among many OUYA games. These features are as follows:

- **Arcade-oriented gameplay**: This typically features simple mechanics that are easy to learn but offer a long progression of mastery
- **Short game sessions/objectives**: These objectives can be completed in less than five minutes but can also be continued if desired
- **Score tracking/leaderboards**: These allow players to see what they've accomplished and compare their score against others

Canabalt gameplay is shown in the following screenshot:

Many of the arcade games out for the OUYA are also available for iPhone or Android or have been ported from them. Canabalt HD is an improved version of the original game for iPhone, remade with 3D graphics for the OUYA. You'll be able to think about mobile development beyond the OUYA as well; the Unity engine has the ability to deploy any game to iOS and Android with minimal tweaks, so you can consider porting your OUYA game to mobile devices.

Touch controls

While you're on the Canabalt HD menu, try making a swipe gesture on the touchpad of the OUYA controller. You will notice that a cursor appears; you can use this cursor to navigate menus. The touchpad can also be used as a secondary jump button while in the game. This functionality is pretty straightforward, but the creative applications of the touchpad are limitless. You could program a sword to slash with a swipe of the touch screen, let a player design custom decals by drawing them with their finger, or use touch input to calculate the direction and velocity of a cannon shot.

Summary

The OUYA console gives hobbyists and independent developers a way to create and play games without having to work through publishers. Every game on the OUYA marketplace is free to download but can include in-game purchasing in order to unlock the full game or new content. The OUYA also has a unique touchpad on its controllers, giving developers more ways to interact with the players. You'll be using the Unity engine to make games which is a versatile yet easily understandable 3D engine that can also deploy to mobile devices such as iPhones and Android phones.

Now that you've gotten to know your console, you're ready to start writing code. As you're working through the programming tutorials in the chapters that follow, don't be afraid to make a backup copy of what you're working on and try coding a mechanic based on the one you find in an existing game on the OUYA marketplace.

In the next chapter, you'll download the Unity3D game engine and configure it to deploy games to your OUYA console.

2
Installing Unity and the OUYA ODK

In the previous chapter, we briefly explained the Unity3D engine, which we'll be using to create games for the OUYA console. In this chapter, you'll link your OUYA to your computer and the Unity development environment, and create a simple workspace to make sure you can deploy and test your coded prototypes using the console.

In this chapter, we will cover the following topics:

- Installing the game engine
- Downloading and configuring additional packages
- Modifying the PATH variable
- Installing packages with the Android SDK
- Configuring the USB connection

Installing the game engine

The first thing we'll do is install the game engine itself. It's a good idea to install Unity first because you'll have to link every other package as and when you download it.

Time for action – setting up Unity

You'll be spending most of your time throughout the course of this book working in the Unity environment, so it's important to get it set up correctly and acclimate yourself with every element of the workspace layout. Perform the following steps to set up Unity:

1. To begin installing Unity, download the installer from `http://unity3d.com/` by clicking on the **Download** tab.

2. Once the download completes, run the installer. It may prompt you with some optional packages to install, including an example project, a web player, and a code editor called **MonoDevelop**.

   The example project and web player aren't necessary as they apply to non-OUYA games, so you can leave them checked or un-check them depending on whether or not you want to explore games on other platforms. However, you'll want to leave **MonoDevelop** checked, as shown in the following screenshot:

   Select components to install:
   - ☑ Unity
   - ☐ Example Project
   - ☐ Unity Development Web Player
   - ☑ MonoDevelop

   Space required: 3.3GB

   If you're using Windows and already use Visual Studio for coding projects, you can also configure Unity to use that as your primary editor in Unity's **Preferences...** menu. Open it from the **Edit** menu, select the **External Tools** tab, and select your installed version of Visual Studio from the drop-down list labeled **External Script Editor**.

   Now that you've got Unity installed, let's take a look at the interface.

3. Start up Unity and click on **New Project** under the **File** menu to choose a place for your first project; for now, just use the default settings because you're only looking around.

> The first time you start Unity, it will prompt you to create a Unity account and choose between the free version of Unity and Unity Pro. Purchasing a Unity Pro license adds several additional features, but you won't need anything more than the free version when it comes to the material in this book.

Unity features several different preset layouts that you can play with to get your workspace exactly how you like it. In the examples in this book, we'll be using the **2 by 3** layout.

4. To change Unity's layout, open the **Window** menu from the top toolbar and open the **Layouts** submenu. Choose the **2 by 3** option and Unity should rearrange itself to look like the following screenshot:

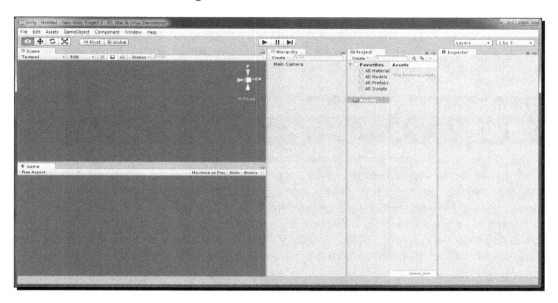

The two stacked windows on the left half of the application are the **Game** and **Scene** windows. The **Game** window will display your game through your main camera, as it will appear to the player. The **Scene** window is a 3D environment that you can move around and view from any angle, and will allow you to interact with the 3D objects in your game.

The three tabs on the right half of your layout are the **Hierarchy**, **Project**, and **Inspector** windows. The **Hierarchy** menu displays all Unity game objects present in the scene, the **Project** menu enables you to navigate your assets so that you can add them to the scene, and the **Inspector** menu lets you change individual properties of a single highlighted object in the **Hierarchy** or **Project** tab. Right now, you don't have any assets, but you have one game object in your **Hierarchy** menu: **Main Camera**. Each empty project will start with this default main camera so it has something to display on the screen, because every game needs at least one camera for the player to view the world through.

What just happened?

You've successfully installed Unity, but it doesn't come ready to develop for OUYA out of the box; next you'll need to link the engine to various packages and dependencies that OUYA uses to communicate with Unity.

Downloading and configuring additional packages

Right now, your Unity installation can only build and run games that are playable on your standalone PC/Mac client. Feel free to exit Unity for now—we'll come back to it when we've downloaded all of the required packages.

Time for action – downloading Java, the Android SDK, and the ODK

The first component we'll need is the **Java Development Kit** (**JDK**) and **Java Runtime Engine** (**JRE**) to handle the Java-side of the OUYA console. Because these are common packages, you may already have them installed on your computer; to check this, open a command line (**Command Prompt** in Windows or **Terminal** in Mac) and type the command `javac -version`. If a version number is displayed, skip over step one of this section and move on to downloading the Android ADT bundle. If you receive an error message that reads "command not found", continue with these steps to install the JDK and JRE.

1. Download and install the JDK and JRE, both of which are available on the Oracle website at `http://www.oracle.com/technetwork/java/javase/ downloads/index.html`.

   The download links will be in the middle of the page, as shown in the following screenshot, with a **Server JRE** download button between them that you can ignore:

2. Once you've downloaded and run the installers, you'll need to download the Android SDK/ADT bundle, which can be found at `http://developer.android.com/sdk/index.html`.

   When installing, you'll want to put everything into a folder called `Development` in your root directory so that if you're using Windows, the full path of the bundle will appear as `C:\Development\adt-bundle-windows-x86_64`. If you're using Mac OS, put it in your home directory so that it appears as `~/Development/adt-bundle-mac-x86_64`. This is important because later, you'll need to change your computer's PATH variable to point to that location.

3. Create a new OUYA developer account by navigating to the developer portal at `https://devs.ouya.tv/developers` and clicking on **Sign in** to download the **OUYA Development Kit**. Click on **Sign up** on the following page and follow the instructions to create your OUYA developer account.

   The **Sign up** button is directly below the login area on the **Sign in** page, as shown in the following screenshot:

4. Finally, download the OUYA Development Kit from the front page of the developer portal. When you unpack it, put it in your `Development` folder so that its path is `Development\OUYA-ODK`.

What just happened?

The Java packages you installed first are necessary for building a game on OUYA, even though you won't be programming in Java; we'll demonstrate the application of the JDK in a later tutorial.

You'll be developing with the API included in the Android SDK/ADT bundle. The OUYA OS is based on Android, which means that there are similarities between it and other devices that run some version of Android. The OUYA Development Kit, on the other hand, is for everything OUYA-specific in development, such as controller input or in-app purchasing. The packages you've downloaded so far are in your `Development` folder, which we will now add to your computer's PATH variable so that the command line recognizes it.

Modifying the PATH variable

Before you issue commands to OUYA from your command line or terminal, you'll need to make sure your system recognizes those commands. To do this, you'll be editing your PATH variable to include the location of the Android SDK you downloaded.

 The PATH variable is a string of directory locations, or paths, that your command line looks through when it's checking for commands. Any commands in directories that are included in your PATH variable can be run from any working directory instead of having to be run from the folder they're stored in.

Mac OS and Windows both have PATH variables, but they're edited differently; the upcoming tutorials will cover both the operations step by step.

Time for action – editing PATH on Mac OS

If you're using Mac OS, your PATH variable can read paths from your `.bash_profile` script. If you aren't familiar with it, you may not have one yet; so in that case, you'll need to create it by performing the following steps:

1. Start up the Terminal and enter `cd ~/` to navigate to your home folder.
2. Type `touch .bash_profile` to create it.
3. Enter `open -e .bash_profile` to open it for editing.

Once you have your bash profile open, add the following lines to it:

```
export ANDROID_HOME="~/Development/adt-bundle-mac-x86_64"
export PATH=$PATH:$ANDROID_HOME/sdk/tools
export PATH=$PATH:$ANDROID_HOME/sdk/platform-tools
```

> If you've changed your default shell from `bash` to a different shell, your profile may be named differently. For instance, if you're using `zsh`, you'll want to edit `~/zshrc` instead of `~/.bash_profile`. Check your shell's documentation for the exact name and location of the profile file.

Now that you've edited your PATH variable, you'll want to refresh it by typing the following command:

```
source ~/.bash_profile
```

To ensure the new directories were added to the PATH variable correctly, write the following line to display the PATH variable:

```
echo $PATH
```

After verifying that your PATH variable contains the directories that we added in this section, prepare for the next step by starting the Android SDK manager with the following command, and then close the Terminal:

```
android sdk
```

What just happened?

You've just edited your PATH variable permanently by adding a few directories to PATH in your profile file, which is loaded every time the computer starts up, so you'll never need to edit it again. Your profile is typically a hidden file starting with a period, and its specific name depends on whatever shell you're running (usually `bash`, by default).

Adding the Android package directories to your PATH variable enables you to send commands to the OUYA console using the Mac OS Terminal, which will be a useful tool when you get into development.

The next tutorial outlines how to make this change on a Windows computer. Feel free to skip over it and advance to the section titled *Installing packages with the Android SDK* if you don't have a Windows computer or don't wish to develop on it at this point in time.

Time for action – editing PATH on Windows

Perform the following steps to edit the PATH variable on Windows:

1. To edit the PATH variable on Windows, right-click on **Computer** and select **Properties**. In the left panel of the **Properties** window, select **Advanced system settings** and click on **Environment Variables....**

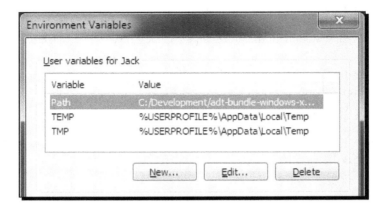

2. In the new window, in the topmost table labeled **User variables**, look for a variable called **Path** or **PATH**. If it exists, click on **Edit...** and add the following code to the end. If it doesn't exist, click on **New...** and create a variable called Path with the following code in it, but omit the preliminary semicolon:

```
C:/Development/adt-bundle-windows-x86-64/sdk/tools;
C:/Development/adt-bundle-windows-x86_64/sdk/platform-tools
```

3. Accept the changes and exit the **Environment Variables** window. To prepare for the next step, open the Android SDK manager by navigating to C:\Development\adt-bundle-windows-x86_64 and running SDK Manager.exe.

What just happened?

The PATH variable on your computer tells your command line where to look for executable commands. Now that you've added the path to the Android SDK to your PATH variable, you can send Android commands to OUYA through the Mac OS Terminal or the Windows Command Prompt.

After adding the proper paths to your PATH variable, you opened the Android SDK manager. Now you'll use this tool to download all of the SDK packages your projects will need.

Installing packages with the Android SDK

Now that you've opened the Android SDK Manager, you'll need to tell it which packages to download so that you have everything the OUYA needs to be recognized by your system. These packages include the main tools of the SDK, the API files for the latest version of Android supported by the OUYA, and the USB driver that your computer needs in order to recognize the OUYA as an Android device.

Time for action – installing Android packages

The SDK manager will give you a list of packages that you can check and install by performing the following steps:

1. Check the following packages:

- ❏ **Android SDK Tools**
- ❏ **Android SDK Platform-tools**
- ❏ **Anroid 4.1.2 (API 16)** platform (except **Google APIs**)
- ❏ **Android Support Library** (in the Extras folder)
- ❏ **Google USB Driver** (in the Extras folder)
- ❏ The following screenshot depicts these packages:

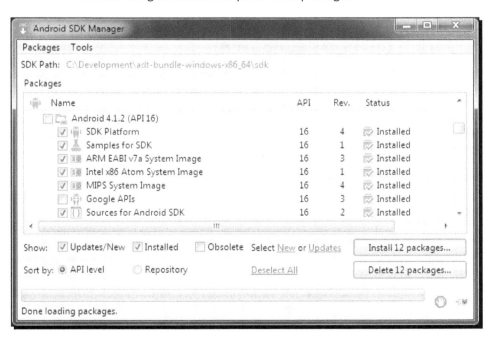

2. After checking all of the packages listed previously, click on **Install 12 packages...** (the total number may vary) and let the SDK manager run its course.

 The future versions of the OUYA software may use a later version of the Android platform. For updated version numbers and instructions, refer to the documentation found at `https://devs.ouya.tv/developers/docs/setup`.

The packages include almost everything we need, but we need to manually configure the Android USB driver before it's ready to use, which is what we'll do next.

What just happened?

The Android SDK Manager is a wide repository of different packages that developers can install, update, and delete. We downloaded a version of Android that wasn't necessarily the most recent version; this is because each Android device is built with a specific supported version, and at the time of writing this, the OUYA supports Version 4.1.2.

As the OUYA software is updated, it's likely to change the supported version. While the installation instructions aren't likely to change much from this book, it is possible that the supported version number will change—updated information can always be found in the documentation on the OUYA developer portal.

Configuring the USB connection

Now is a good time to connect your OUYA to the computer and establish a connection between the two. Use a micro USB-to-USB cable to connect them together and press the power button on the top of the OUYA to turn it on.

You can verify that the device is connected by running the following three commands in succession:

```
android update adb
adb kill-server
adb devices
```

If the OUYA is powered on and connected, you should see it represented as a string of seemingly random characters in the device list. However, because the OUYA is a unique device, the driver information that you downloaded with the SDK manager may not have everything it needs to properly detect the OUYA when it's connected to your computer. To fix this, we'll have to manually insert an entry for OUYA into the driver file. Note that this step is only necessary if you're running a Windows operating system; if you're developing for OUYA on a Mac, this won't be an issue and your OUYA will connect without any additional configuration.

Time for action – configuring the USB driver on Windows

The file we need to edit on Windows operating systems is found at `C:\Development\adt-bundle-windows-x86_64\sdk\extras\google\usb_driver\android_winusb.inf`. Perform the following steps to edit the driver file:

1. Double-click on the file to open it in Notepad and find the section that begins with `[Google.NTx86]`. You'll see a list of devices already below this header; after the last device, add the highlighted text shown in the following screenshot:

```
android_winusb.inf - Notepad
File  Edit  Format  View  Help
[Google.NTx86]

;Google Nexus One
%SingleAdbInterface%         = USB_Install, USB\VID_18D1&PID_0D02
%CompositeAdbInterface%      = USB_Install, USB\VID_18D1&PID_0D02&MI_01
%SingleAdbInterface%         = USB_Install, USB\VID_18D1&PID_4E11
%CompositeAdbInterface%      = USB_Install, USB\VID_18D1&PID_4E12&MI_01

;Google Nexus S
%SingleAdbInterface%         = USB_Install, USB\VID_18D1&PID_4E21
%CompositeAdbInterface%      = USB_Install, USB\VID_18D1&PID_4E22&MI_01
%SingleAdbInterface%         = USB_Install, USB\VID_18D1&PID_4E23
%CompositeAdbInterface%      = USB_Install, USB\VID_18D1&PID_4E24&MI_01

;Google Nexus 7
%SingleBootLoaderInterface%  = USB_Install, USB\VID_18D1&PID_4E40
%CompositeAdbInterface%      = USB_Install, USB\VID_18D1&PID_4E42&MI_01
%CompositeAdbInterface%      = USB_Install, USB\VID_18D1&PID_4E44&MI_01

;Google Nexus Q
%SingleBootLoaderInterface%  = USB_Install, USB\VID_18D1&PID_2C10
%SingleAdbInterface%         = USB_Install, USB\VID_18D1&PID_2C11

;Google Nexus (generic)
%SingleBootLoaderInterface%  = USB_Install, USB\VID_18D1&PID_4EE0
%CompositeAdbInterface%      = USB_Install, USB\VID_18D1&PID_4EE2&MI_01
%CompositeAdbInterface%      = USB_Install, USB\VID_18D1&PID_4EE4&MI_02
%CompositeAdbInterface%      = USB_Install, USB\VID_18D1&PID_4EE6&MI_01

;OUYA Console
%SingleAdbInterface% = USB_Install, USB\VID_2836&PID_0010
%CompositeAdbInterface% = USB_Install, USB\VID_2836&PID_0010&MI_01
```

2. Add the same block of text in the same place under the similar section `[Google.NTamd64]`, then save the document, and close Notepad.

> The values that you entered shouldn't have a blank space after them, including any spaces or returns. Make sure that each line ends with the final character to avoid errors.

3. Next, open the Windows Command Prompt and run the following commands:

```
adb kill-server
echo 0x2836 >> "%USERPROFILE%\.android\adb_usb.ini"
adb start-server
```

4. Close the command prompt and right-click on **Computer** in your **Start** menu. Select **Properties**, and in the window that opens select **Device Manager**. Locate the **OUYA Console** on the list—most likely under **Portable Devices**—right-click on it and select **Update Driver Software...**, as shown in the following screenshot:

5. Choose **Browse my computer** for the driver software and then select **Let me pick from a list of device drivers on my computer**. Click on **Show All Devices** if available and then on **Have Disk** on the resulting screen. Navigate to the directory that contains your edited driver file, accept the driver, and exit. Your computer is now ready to recognize your console.

 Your computer may warn you that the device driver isn't signed. In this case, you can go ahead and ignore it because the driver is safe. The fact that the driver is unsigned is the reason we had to manually point to its location, but other than that it won't have any impact on what you need to do.

What just happened?

You downloaded the USB driver for general Android devices, but the driver needed a little more tweaking before it was ready to communicate with the OUYA. To fix this, you added an OUYA entry to the driver, making it recognizable by your computer.

Having the correct drivers is important because you'll be sending code from your Unity development environment directly to the OUYA console to build and debug via USB, and without that additional entry in the driver file it would result in an error.

Time for action – exporting OUYA packages from Unity

The last thing you need before you can link everything you've downloaded to Unity is the Unity OUYA plugin. This can be downloaded directly from the developers at `https://github.com/ouya/ouya-unity-plugin`. Perform the following steps to install the plugin:

1. Click on the button on the page that says **Download ZIP** and put it in a location that's easy to find. When it has downloaded, unzip the archive and open Unity.

2. In the **Unity** window, navigate to **File | Open Project...**, browse the unzipped folder, and click on **Open**. On Mac OS, you may need to click on **Open Other...** to access the folder's location.

    Depending on the latest versions of Unity and the plugin, you may be prompted to upgrade the project to work with the latest version of Unity. If it does, then accept the prompt; if you don't receive the prompt, it will work fine as it is.

    After opening the plugin files as a project, two new drop-down lists will appear on the top toolbar of Unity: **OUYA** and **NGUI**.

3. Open the **OUYA** menu and click on **Export Core Package**, as shown in the following screenshot, to save the core package as a Unity package file that you can import into all of your projects:

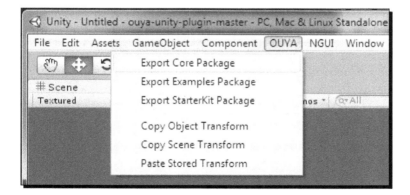

When exporting packages from Unity, the package files will always be found in the root directory of the project, which in this case is your `ouya-unity-plugin-master` directory.

4. Repeat this process for the other two packages until you have all three exported together. You only need the **Core Package**, but the others serve as a good reference for your own learning.

   You'll import these exported packages into any project that you develop for the OUYA, so it's a good idea to keep them handy.

5. Save a copy of your exported packages to your `Development` folder in your root or home directory so that you can access them easily later.

It's also a good idea to copy the NGUI package from `ouya-unity-plugin-master/Assets/NGUI` to the same place, as it's helpful to a lot of Unity's features (particularly the user interface). However, you won't be required to use NGUI in any of the prototypes or games you develop in this book.

What just happened?

You just exported all of the required OUYA packages from the ODK project, which you'll now be able to import into any new project to set it up for deployment on the OUYA. If you ever lose these packages or want to update them to a new version of the OUYA SDK, simply re-export the packages from the `ouya-unity-plugin-masters` project again.

Time for action – importing packages into a new workspace

Now that you have all of the packages required for OUYA development, you can import them into the Unity workspace by performing the following steps:

1. Start a new project in Unity and double-click on the core package you exported to import it into your workspace. Unity will prompt you with a list of possible items to import; make sure they're all checked and click on **Import**. The OUYA menu will re-appear along the top toolbar as soon as the import completes.

2. Open the **Window** menu along that toolbar and click on **Open OUYA Panel**.

3. This window is where we'll finally link all of the packages we've downloaded so far to the engine. The panel also has a space to link an NDK, which we will download and link to last.

4. The **Unity** tab will automatically contain what it needs, so first click on the **Java JDK** tab and browse to the location of your JDK, as shown in the following screenshot:

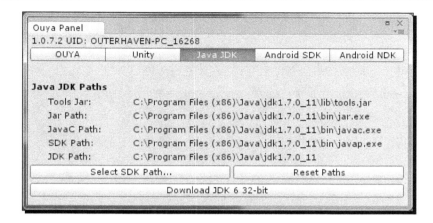

5. Next, click on the **Android SDK** tab and do the same. Note that it may not be as automatic as the Java process as the locations of files in the SDK tend to change; if that happens, locate the files at their new location and move them to the potential locations displayed in gray. As long as you downloaded all of the packages listed earlier in the chapter, you have the files; they just might not be in the place Unity expects them to be.

6. Also, check the **minSDKVersion** value that's at the top of the **Android SDK** tab. If it's not set to **16** (currently the supported SDK version for OUYA), you'll have to click on **Edit**, then move the mouse over **Project Settings** and click on **Player**. This will display your player settings in the **Inspector** window on the right-most pane of the Unity environment, where you can change the **Minimum API Level** to **16** (Android 4.1) under the **Other Settings** tab. Make sure you're viewing the **Android** tab at the top of the **Inspector** window:

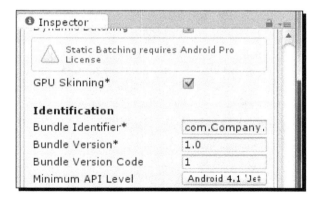

Once every path to the Android SDK is set, you just need to download and link to the Android NDK. The Android NDK tab has a link at the bottom to download the required package.

7. Download the proper version from the site it opens and store it in your development folder so that its path is `Development/android-ndk-r8d`. Link to this location in the **OUYA panel** window, as shown in the following screenshot, by browsing to that location and it should find the necessary files automatically.

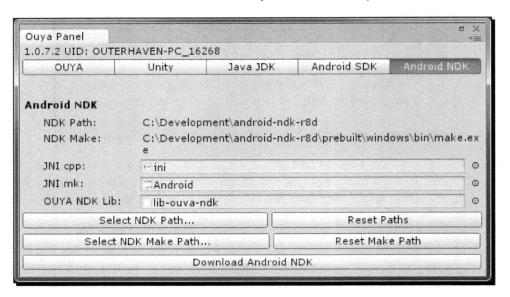

What just happened?

The last step in setting up your development environment is linking your engine to the API that you'll be working in. The OUYA panel that you added to Unity using the OUYA Unity plugin serves as a sort of checklist organized into tabs, making sure you have every package necessary to build to the OUYA. The Java JDK is necessary for Unity and the Android SDK Manager to run. The Android SDK is the main package, as it includes code necessary for any project to run on Android.

The NDK that you downloaded and linked is a secondary Android package that isn't always necessary for Android projects but will be for OUYA projects. It enables the execution of low-level code that we won't need to deal with but is still necessary for "under-the-hood" operations. The following table lists various packages and their purpose:

Package names	Purpose
Java JDK	It provides a framework for Unity and the Android SDK manager.
Android SDK	This is the bulk of the Android API that the OUYA uses (along with every other Android device).

Package names	Purpose
Ouya ODK	This includes the OUYA-specific components of the API, including controller input and other game mechanics.
Android NDK	This is an optional Android package. Not all Android projects need it, but Unity uses it to deploy to the OUYA.

Pop quiz – small parts of a whole

Q1. What should the minimum API level of your Unity Android project be to properly deploy to the OUYA?

1. API level 18 (Android 4.3)
2. API level 11 (Android 3.0)
3. API level 16 (Android 4.1)
4. API level 15 (Android 4.0.3)

Q2. What package needs to be imported in order to display the OUYA panel in the Unity workspace?

1. StarterKit Package
2. Core Package
3. Examples Package
4. NGUI Package

Summary

At long last, the linking is complete! Give yourself a pat on the back for getting through the dull part. Even though you haven't done any development yet, all of the packages that you downloaded, configured, and linked to Unity will allow you to deploy your code to run on your OUYA console natively at any time, which is an important step in creating software for an external device. Save the project as it is so that you have a linked project ready to go for the next chapter where you'll begin programming and testing.

3
Diving into Development

In the last two chapters, you familiarized yourself with the Unity development environment and had a taste of what you can create for the OUYA. Now it's time for the fun part: creating code that turns your ideas into mechanics. In this chapter, you'll create your first functioning prototype and write some basic code to see action on the screen. In doing this, you'll cover basic gameplay scripting techniques and some introductory programming in the C# language. We'll also look at the tools provided to us in the Unity API.

Specifically, we'll cover the following topics:

- Setting up a scene in Unity
- Navigating the scene in your workspace
- Lighting and cameras
- Adding scripts to objects

If you're already familiar with Unity and the fundamentals of scripting in C#, feel free to advance to the next chapter; nothing in this chapter is built upon in future chapters, it's only for getting you up to speed with the basic tools we'll be using.

Creating a 3D text prototype

We're going to build a simple 3D text prototype that changes color when triggered by user input. To begin with, either create a new project configured for the OUYA (as demonstrated in *Chapter 2*, *Installing Unity and the OUYA ODK*) or simply use the project that you created while following along with this book.

Time for action – manipulating the scene

When you've opened your project, you'll notice that there's only one object in your **Hierarchy** menu by default; the **Main Camera** object, which projects the game screen. Now perform the following steps:

1. Select that camera by clicking on it in the **Hierarchy** menu once. While the camera is selected, you can see an outline of its view plane in the **Scene** window.

Think of the camera in Unity as a cameraman on a movie set. Everything he sees ends up on the screen, and if something is out of his view, it doesn't make it into the movie. As a developer, you can see everything in your Unity scene at all times, but when you publish your game, the player will only be able to see what the camera captures. Don't worry about this yet—we'll get into camera programming later.

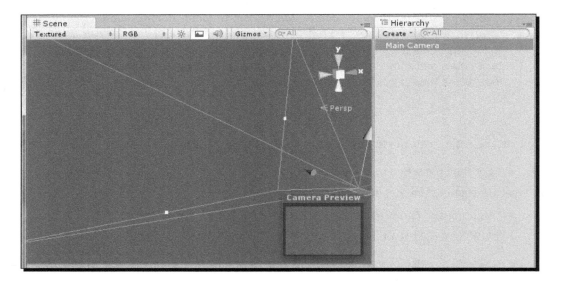

You'll also notice that while the camera is selected, there are three colored arrows pointing in different directions from the camera's origin. These arrows represent the three axes of position in the game world.

2. Click-and-drag on these arrows to move the camera back and forth on their respective axes. If you grab the camera from the center cube, you can move it across all three axes at the same time. All other game objects can be moved with this same method.

Notice the values in the **Inspector** window while you drag the camera. As you move it through the game world, its coordinates update in the **Transform** pane. Alternatively, you can enter a set of coordinates manually into the position axes, and the selected object will move to those coordinates in the scene.

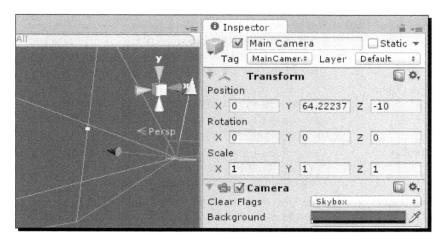

Moving objects in your scene isn't too helpful from just a single perspective, so Unity has keyboard controls to navigate all dimensions of your scene.

To enter the navigation mode, hold down your right mouse button while your cursor is over the **Scene** view. You can move the mouse while the button is held down to look around, or use the *W*, *A*, *S*, and *D* keys to move forward, left, backwards, and right, respectively. You can also move upwards with the *E* key and downwards with the *Q* key. If you wish to move faster at any time, holding down the *Shift* key will increase your speed.

Moving around in an empty world isn't going to do anything for us, so let's add some objects to the scene. Before we can see any physical object clearly, we need to light the scene, so a light will be the first object we add.

3. At the top of your **Hierarchy** window, there's a button labeled **Create**. Click on it and select **Directional Light** from the drop-down menu. Your light will then appear in the **Hierarchy** and **Scene** views, with outlines to show the orientation of the light.

We picked a directional light because it's a simple and fast way to light any scene, but there are four main types of lights in Unity that offer their own uses. They are as listed in the following table:

Light type	Behavior
Directional Light	This shines light universally in a certain direction. The position of these lights in a scene doesn't matter because they illuminate the entire scene evenly, but the angle changes the way the light hits the scene.
Point Light	This emits light from a single point in all directions. Their rotation doesn't matter because the light is emitted evenly from the origin, but the position compared to other objects in the scene affects how strongly it lights them.
Spotlight	This projects a cone of light from an origin towards a certain direction. Rotation and position both matter because the luminosity and orientation angles are both finite.
Area Light	Area lights shine in all directions to one side of a plane and are typically used to light scenes with realistic detail. Currently, they are only available with an upgrade to Unity Pro, and you will not need to use them throughout the course of this book.

Each light also has its own individual properties that can be changed in the **Inspector** menu. These properties include **Color**, **Intensity**, **Shadow Type**, and so on. Once you've set up a scene, don't be afraid to play with light settings and watch the game world change in real time in the **Scene** window.

You now have an empty, lit world and you're ready to fill it with physical objects.

4. Go back to the **Create** button at the top of the **Hierarchy** window and select **Plane**. Set every position axis to 0 in the **Inspector** window so that the plane is in the middle of the scene, and then set your camera's **X**, **Y**, and **Z** position axes to 0, 2.5, and -10 so it has a good view of the plane we placed.

When you're finished, your environment should look something like as shown in the following screenshot (your **Scene** view will vary based on where you positioned it):

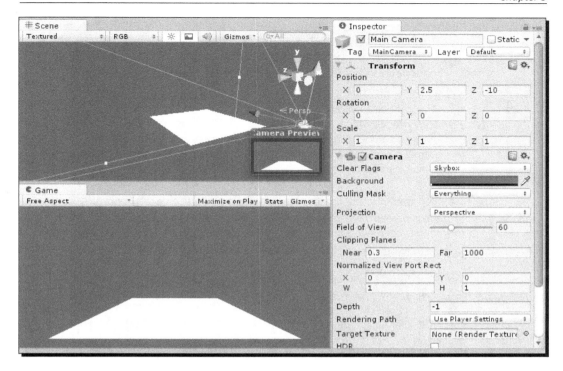

What just happened?

Thoroughly remember the steps you just performed, because it's how you'll start every project in Unity. Cameras and lighting may not be things we actively notice in games, but they're of paramount importance in Unity. Without them, everything we'd see would be dark or out of the frame, which isn't a suitable stage for your creations.

Time for action – creating and scripting 3D text

To demonstrate basic object properties in Unity, we'll create a 3D text object, which is a kind of game object that displays a string of text at a point in 3D space. The positions of all game objects are specified in X, Y, and Z coordinates, and each coordinate can be changed individually in the **Inspector** window. Now, perform the following steps:

1. Open the **Create** menu and select **3D Text** to create a **New Text** object.

2. Use the **Inspector** window to position it at 0, 5, and 0, and then set the **Anchor** dropdown to **middle center** and the **Alignment** dropdown to **center**.

This puts your text directly in the center of the scene, elevated above the plane. The default text is **Hello World**, which is a common filler phase that developers enter when they are first testing text and display. This can be changed to any text you enter in the **Inspector** window under the **Text Mesh** pane.

Every object inspector window is an aggregation of all the object's components, which are organized into panes. Most objects share some components, such as **Transform** (position) and **Mesh Renderer** (appearance), but additional components are the ones that define an object's attributes and abilities.

Any displayed text in Unity can also be changed while the game is running by attaching a code script, which is what we'll do next. Make sure your scene is still positioned in the way we placed it previously, which should look as shown in the following screenshot through your **Game** window's main camera view:

Now is a good time to save your progress before we start writing code.

3. Click on **File** and then **Save Scene**. The default save location will be your project's `Assets` folder, but it's a good practice to keep your `Assets` folder organized into subfolders, so create a new folder called `Scenes` and save your scene within it as `3dtext`. Your new folder will immediately appear inside your **Project** window below the `Assets` folder, with your scene inside.

Saving your scene isn't the same as saving your project; your project's saved files only store information about where different component files are stored (assets, scripts, and so on), while your scene's saved data tells the engine how everything is actually positioned within the scene. Think of your project files as useful information for your operating system, and your scene files as useful information for Unity.

Your scene is set up, saved, and ready for scripts, so we'll now begin coding by creating a C# script that controls the color of the text object.

4. Right-click on your `Assets` folder and create another subfolder called `Scripts`.

5. Right-click on the `Scripts` folder, move your mouse over **Create**, and select **C# Script** from the drop-down menu.

By creating files from a folder's **Create** menu, they'll be created within that folder automatically.

6. Name the script `ColorChanger` and double-click on it to open it in your code editor.

Before we start adding code to the script, we'll do a quick explanation of the anatomy of a script, including all of the important keywords that you need to know and what they mean.

The first two lines of the script that begin with the `using` keyword denote the code libraries that this script relies on. Just below these is your script's **class definition**, which gives the code compiler basic information about the script.

Keep in mind that your class name needs to match the script name in order for Unity to load it correctly. If you rename the script file from the **Project** window or manually in your filesystem in the future, the class name won't update automatically within the script, so make sure they match in order to avoid getting an error.

The `public` keyword means that other scripts can interact with this one, and the `MonoBehavior` keyword is the name of the built-in script this one inherits basic properties from. The bracket after the `inheritance` keyword and the bracket at the very end of the script encapsulate the entire class, and most of your code will be contained between these brackets. It is possible to write code for a class in a separate script if the situation calls for it, but you won't need to do that for the projects in this book.

Every Unity script has two functions already defined in the code when you create it: the `Start` function and the `Update` function. Functions are blocks of executable code that can be called to run by the game engine. The `Start` function is automatically called when an object with this script attached first enters the scene. The `Update` function is called for every frame, which is extremely quick (typically around 60 times per second), and it manages how the scripted object changes over the passage of time. There are several other built-in functions in Unity's API that can be extended in code by adding the function to a script, and you can create functions from scratch that execute your own code as well.

Both of your starting functions have plain English descriptions written above them. The compiler doesn't interpret these descriptions, but they can be helpful for the programmer to keep notes; any text can be marked as a comment by inserting two forward slashes before it.

Notice that each of the pre-existing functions have parentheses and brackets directly after their names and the word void before them. The word before the function name represents the type of data that the function can return to; void means it won't be sending any data back to the caller. Other common return types include `int` (integer number), `bool` (true or false), and `string` (readable text).

The parentheses after the function name serve a purpose similar to the `return` keyword, but in the opposite direction; whatever is inside the parentheses denote data that must be sent to the function from the caller. The two pre-existing functions don't have anything inside the parentheses because they don't require data to be passed to them to function.

Lastly, the brackets after the input parameter parentheses are the boundaries of the function. All code that the function contains goes between these two brackets, almost always separated by several lines. Right now, the brackets don't have anything inside of them, and that's what we're going to fill in now.

7. Write a new line, as shown in the following code, with an explanatory comment in your `Start` function that will change the color of the text material to red:

```
void Start ()
{
  //change the object's color to red
  gameObject.renderer.material.color = Color.red;
}
```

Downloading the example code

You can download the example code files for all Packt books you have purchased from your account at http://www.packtpub.com. If you purchased this book elsewhere, you can visit http://www.packtpub.com/support and register to have the files e-mailed directly to you.

The preceding line of code refers to `gameObject`, which represents the object that we attached the script to. It then points to renderer, a component of said object, and changes the rendered material's color to the standard `Color.red`. Each line of non-commented code is terminated with a semicolon to tell the compiler to move on to the next line. Make sure each statement ends with a semicolon to avoid compiler errors.

You're not expected to know these commands and keywords already; even if you've had experience with C#, coding in Unity is unique to the engine. You'll develop a natural memory of different code elements in Unity, but if you ever forget something, the Unity web documentation contains every function and keyword in the API.

Save your code in the **File** menu of your code editor to make sure all of your additions to the script were applied. The code will do what we want it to, but it still doesn't know which object we want to run it on; link the code file to your 3D text object by dragging it from your **Project** window onto the text object in your **Hierarchy** window. Alternatively, you can click on the **Add Component** button at the bottom of the item's **Inspector** window and find the `ColorChanger` script under the **Scripts** tab. If you select the text object, you'll see that the script is a newly added component in the **Inspector** window.

Press the play arrow button (seen in the following screenshot) at the top of the Unity editor window to see your scene in action. The play button is useful because you can test right in the editor without having to deploy to the console. As soon as your game starts, your 3D text object will turn red according to the script we attached to it.

What just happened?

You're on the road to code! Every script in Unity is created from a basic template in the **Project** window, edited in a code editor, and linked to an object in your **Hierarchy** window by clicking-and-dragging. Scripts can be applied to any number of objects, but be careful that you don't attach scripts to objects that lack the attributes the code looks for. For instance, if you were to try to change the color of the camera, the engine would return an error, because the camera isn't a visible object, and thus doesn't have a renderer.

The names of functions and variables that you create are completely up to you, but many programmers follow a few common conventions to avoid confusion. In the Unity API, variables are camel case (first word all lowercase, first letter of all following words capitalized, as in `mainPlayerPosition`). Unlike variables, every word in function names is usually capitalized, as in `MovePlayerForward()`.

Have a go hero – flexing your new muscle

Now that you've got the basics down, play around with your new talent. A large part of programming and game development is finding out what works for you and what doesn't. Change small things at first as you start to learn the natural flow of coding, and make bigger changes if it starts to seem too easy. Here are some ideas to get you started:

◆ Explore the different available colors

◆ Attach your `ColorChanger` script to the plane object

◆ Explore the different attributes that your editor's code hinting suggests

◆ Add a function to the script by copying the built-in function format

If you develop a taste for exploring on your own, look over some of the beginner topics in online question/answer forums on the web, such as `www.stackoverflow.com`.

You can also learn straight from the source by following Unity's beginner tutorials, found at `http://unity3d.com/learn`.

Creating a custom function

The `Start` function of any script is great for initializing the object's first values, but most scripts rely on several custom functions that get called more than once, and potentially many times.

Time for action – writing a function

In this tutorial, you'll begin writing your own functions and calling them to be executed. Perform the following steps to write a function:

1. Create a new script in the same way you created the color-changing script, but name it `ObjectMover`. Open the script and add the function declaration named `MoveObject` below the declaration for `Update`, so that your full code file appears as shown in the following code:

```
using UnityEngine;
using System.Collections;

public class ObjectMover : MonoBehaviour
{
    //use this for initialization
```

```
void Start ()
{

}

//Update is called once per frame
void Update ()
{

}

void MoveObject ()
{

}
}
```

You've now declared a brand-new function, as simple as that.

2. Next, add the following line of code that will make it move positively along the *x* axis (to the right) by two units:

```
Void MoveObject ()
{
    gameObject.transform.Translate(2.0f, 0.0f, 0.0f);
}
```

The parentheses at the end of this line tell us that a function is being called, and the information inside of them is what's required for that function to run. In this case, we're calling the `Translate` function, which receives three numeric values that are each applied to the *x*, *y*, and *z* axes of the object we're moving. If we tried to call this function without those parameters, we would receive an error.

> When we edited the color of the text, we didn't need to call a function because we could just assign our color value directly to the attribute. More complicated procedures such as moving an object through 3D space require a function to serve as a list of steps in a process. We can assign a value to an attribute by simply using the equal to sign that has the new value after it, but if you're calling a function, you must include the parentheses and the required parameters.

Our `MoveObject` function is ready to go; all we need to do is call it. The `Start` and `Update` functions run automatically, but other functions need to be called for execution. Fortunately, because the `Start` function runs automatically, we can have it call our new function.

3. Add the following call to your `Start` function:

```
Void Start ()
{
  MoveObject();
}
```

Save your changes and attach your new script to your text object. The `ObjectMover` script has now been added as a component in addition to the `ColorChanger` script, and we put a function call for it in the `Start` function so that it will be called as soon as it's loaded.

4. Click on the play arrow button at the top of the editor window to see your new function in action, as shown in the following screenshot:

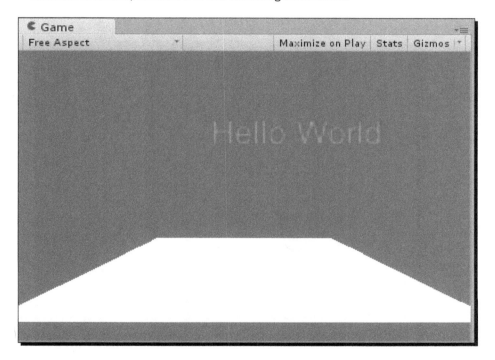

As expected, the text immediately moves two units to the right and creates a visible offset from the center of the plane. We don't see movement because we haven't programmed any animations or gradual changes yet; we only have a function that moves text immediately and is called once. But what if we were to call it twice?

5. Edit your `Start` code to call the `MoveObject` function again, as shown in the following code:

```
Void Start ()
{
  MoveObject();
  MoveObject();
}
```

If you save your changes and run it, you'll see that the distance the text moves has doubled, because we ran the same operation twice.

As you can see in the following screenshot, the text has moved further on the screen than when we called the function once:

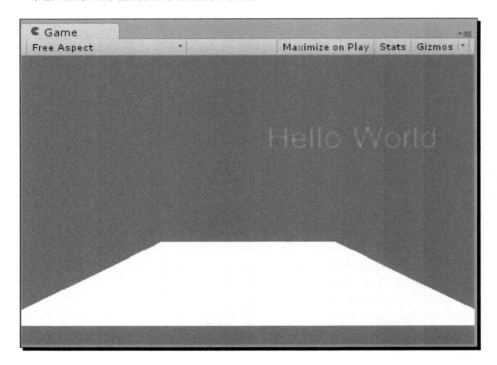

Functions can be called as frequently or as infrequently as you want, and it's good practice to write your functions in such a way that calls to it would apply in several situations, so that you don't have to write multiple overly specific functions.

Object-oriented programming (OOP) is a programming practice that partly involves writing code that can be reused as much as possible. Having broad functions that handle many situations well can save a lot of time and effort.

Next, we'll add some functionality to the script's `Update` function. So far, we've only made calls from our `Start` function. The `Start` function only runs once, so we can't see any changes from it. The `Update` function that we've been seeing gets called once per frame, and we can use that frequency to simulate real-time passing.

6. Remove both calls to `MoveObject` from the `Start` function and put one call in the `Update` function, as shown in the following code:

```
void Update ()
{
  MoveObject();
}
```

If we were to run this program right now, our 3D text would be out of the frame before our eyes could even see it; calling that function twice was enough to create an obvious visible difference, but in the `Update` function, it would be called twice in a fraction of a second.

7. To compensate, let's decrease the amount that the text is moved by `0.01f` units using the following code:

```
Void MoveObject ()
{
  gameObject.transform.Translate(0.01f, 0.0f, 0.0f);
}
```

If `0.01f` seems small, that's because it is, but it will add up very quickly if it's called for every frame, and the movement will appear smooth because it's so subtle.

 The f character found after the parameter values of the `Translate` function denotes a float or floating point number. Unlike an integer, floats can hold numbers with decimals. C# requires the f character after every float, and the code will cause an error if it's omitted.

Press the play arrow button and observe the text moving along the *x* axis by 0.01 units every frame or approximately 60 times per second. Most animations, gradual motions, and timings in games are programmed with frame-by-frame functions, so remember to consider this when creating your mechanics.

What just happened?

By writing your own function from scratch in the `ObjectMover` script, you've begun to dictate the behavior of any object that it's attached to. Most of the functionality in your games will be written with your own functions, but the built-in `Start` function lets you call things from the start of the game, and the `Update` function lets you keep things moving every frame.

Time for action – capturing data with return values

What's on the outside of your functions matters just as much as what's on the inside. Optimizing the amount of information passed around between functions ensures that you'll never find a bridge that you can't code across. Perform the following steps to capture data:

1. Move your function call from the `Update` function back to the `Start` function and reset the translation value to `2.0f`. For learning purposes, imagine that your `Start` function needs to know how far the `MoveObject` function moved the text to the right. We already know that the movement value is a float, so we can change the return type from `void` to `float`. Your function should now look like the one shown in the following code:

```
float MoveObject ()
{
   gameObject.transform.Translate(2.0f, 0.0f, 0.0f);
}
```

 At this point, the `MoveObject` function will cause an error because nothing is explicitly returned in the function body. Using a return type in a function necessitates a return, so you'll only want a non-void return type when you're returning valid data every time the function is called. For functions that only offer valid data sometimes, you might consider using a `void` return type and updating the value of a variable instead.

Now we're faced with two purposes for the translation value instead of just one: we want to apply the value to a translation, and we want to send it back to the caller. If a value is needed more than once, it's a good practice to create a variable. Variables are data that you name and define the type of; they hold a value that can be referred to anytime.

2. Declare and initialize a variable to represent our translation value, as shown in the following code:

```
float MoveObject ()
{
   float translationValue = 2.0f;
```

```
    gameObject.transform.Translate(translationValue, 0.0f, 0.0f);
}
```

We declared the variable type first, followed by the name, and then we immediately assigned it a value of `2.0f` with the equal to operand. After our variable has a value, we can use it anywhere we would have used `2.0f`, such as the X parameter of the `Translate` function.

3. Add a line to return that same value using your variable and satisfy the requirement for a returned float, as shown in the following code:

```
float MoveObject ()
{
  float translationValue = 2.0f;
  gameObject.transform.Translate(translationValue, 0.0f, 0.0f);
  return translationValue;
}
```

Return lines are often the last lines in code blocks because returning a value terminates a function, even if there is code after the return within the same function. You'll get more acquainted with early returns a little later when you're making conditional statements, but always be careful about putting code after a return, because it may never be called.

We can now test the return by reading it in the `Start` function. For testing purposes, we'll use Unity's print command, a simple way to display data feedback in the bottom-left corner of the development window.

4. Modify your existing function call, as shown in the following code, by instructing it to print out the results:

```
void Start ()
{
  print(MoveObject());
}
```

We put the `MoveObject` function call inside the print function call, because we wanted to print whatever the result of the `MoveObject` function is. Save your changes and press the play arrow button and you'll see the number **2** displayed in the log area at the bottom-left, being read by the `print` function from the return value.

What just happened?

Often, having a function that simply runs its code and then terminates isn't enough. We need to read values from that function to see what it did, observe changes, and inform other systems about their status. By setting a return value on the function, we let the function talk back to the caller, establishing shared data that can help move a game along quickly.

 Putting a return type in a function can sometimes be a double-edged sword; often, returning values is easy and helpful, but since having a return type mandates a return no matter what, you may have to bend more complicated functions to return the data you want, no matter what the circumstances.

Time for action – controlling functions with parameters

Our functions now communicate back to us, but we still haven't communicated to our functions; that's where input parameters come in. Declaring parameters in your function declaration requires the presence of one or many values, without which it couldn't function. For instance, if we wanted our `MoveObject` function to move the target game object to a different distance each time we called it, we could make that distance one of the required parameters, so each function calling `MoveObject` will need to tell it how far to translate. Perform the following steps for controlling functions with parameters:

1. Remove the declaration for `translationValue` on the top line of the `MoveObject` function and declare a distance parameter, as shown in the following code:

```
float MoveObject ( float translationValue )
{
  gameObject.transform.Translate(translationValue, 0.0f, 0.0f);
  return translationValue;
}
```

We can still refer to the variable `translationValue` because it's been declared in the parameters instead of the function body, which means the value will come from the function caller instead of the function itself. This also means that we'll have to send the value when the function is called in `Start`.

2. Input the value of `2.0f` into the call. Also, remove the `print` function call for now, as shown in the following code:

```
void Start ()
{
  MoveObject(2.0f);
}
```

Keep in mind that we could also have called this function with a variable, similar to what we did when we declared `translationValue` inside of `MoveObject`. We can even pass in a variable declared in `Start`, as shown in the following code:

```
void Start ()
{
  float distanceToTranslate = 2.0f;
  MoveObject(distanceToTranslate);
}
```

The name of the variable passed in to the function doesn't have to match the name of the parameter declaration, but the function being called will always access passed data using the parameter name.

You're not limited to one parameter when declaring a function. Functions can carry out many operations at a time on multiple things that are passed in. To demonstrate, we'll add a text parameter to `MoveObject`, in addition to the distance parameter, and have it print out the value to the log before returning.

3. Add a second parameter of type `string` and name it `textToDisplay`. Then, add a line before the return to print its contents to the log. The code is as follows:

```
float MoveObject ( float translationValue,
  string textToDisplay )
{
  gameObject.transform.Translate(translationValue, 0.0f, 0.0f);
  print(textToDisplay);
  return translationValue;
}
```

4. Now, alter your call to `MoveObject` in `Start` so that it provides both required parameters. Note that string values must be contained in quotes.

```
void Start ()
{
  float distanceToTranslate = 2.0f;
  string textToDisplay = "Hello World!"
  MoveObject(distanceToTranslate, textToDisplay);
}
```

Hit the play button after saving your changes and watch the bottom status bar for your string message, which is **Hello World!**.

What just happened?

Now that you understand return types and function parameters, you can send all sorts of data to and from each function in your script. Single functions make changes, but many functions make games. Learning to establish an exchange of information at every opportunity will let your individual systems shine as a cohesive whole.

Now that you've taken your first steps in scripting, we'll tie everything together by designating a key on the keyboard to call a function that changes the color of your text and returns the current position of the text in the Vector3 format.

Making our scripts interactive

In order for a script to behave based on user input, it needs to be constantly checking for changes in the keyboard state. As this can be considered a perpetual system, we'll use the Update function, which, as you may recall, is called with every frame automatically.

Time for action – adding keyboard interaction to scripts

Perform the following steps to add keyboard interaction to your scripts:

1. Add the following if statement to your Update function that checks if the *Return* key is pressed:

```
// Update is called once per frame
void Update()
{
  if(Input.GetKeyDown(KeyCode.Return))
  {

  }
}
```

Everything contained within the if statement will run every time the Update function detects that the *Return* key has just been pressed down (there's a slightly different way to check if a key is being held down, but we'll cover that in the next chapter).

We could add code directly inside the if statement to change the color of the text, but it's better to write a function for an action like that in case you want to replicate the same functionality outside of that if statement without writing redundant code, so we'll create a dedicated ChangeColor function.

2. Declare the `ChangeColor` function below the `Update` function in your `ColorChanger` script, as shown in the following code:

```
void Update()
{
    if(Input.GetKeyDown(KeyCode.Return))
    {

    }
}


Vector3 ChangeColor(Color newColor)
{

}
```

Note that our new function has a `Color` parameter so we can pass in any color we want the text to change to, and it has a `Vector3` return value so we can retrieve the object's position the moment the function is called.

> Typically, a function's return value is related in some way to the operation it performs, which isn't the case with our coloring function returning a position. We're only returning the position as a way to test drive return values; later in the book, we'll incorporate more applicable return values that provide useful information about the status of a function or its end result.

3. Add the following line to your `ChangeColor` function to assign the passed-in color to the text object:

```
Vector3 ChangeColor(Color newColor)
{
    gameObject.renderer.material.color = newColor;
}
```

4. Next, add a line that returns the object's current position, as shown in the following code:

```
Vector3 ChangeColor(Color newColor)
{
    gameObject.renderer.material.color = newColor;
    return gameObject.transform.position;
}
```

5. Now, your function is ready to be called, so add a call to the `if` statement you wrote in the `Update` function that changes the object's color to green:

```
void Update()
{
  if(Input.GetkeyDown(KeyCode.Return))
  {
    ChangeColor(Color.green);
  }
}
```

6. Press the play button in the Unity editor to test your new function.

    The text should still appear red when it begins because you're still setting the color to red in the `Start` function, but as soon as you press the *Return* key, the text color will change to green, as shown in the following screenshot:

    Next, we'll add another `if` statement to check a different key that will change the text to a different color, to demonstrate the dynamic nature of our `Color` parameter.

7. Add the following `if` statement to your `Update` function:

```
void Update()
{
```

```
if(Input.GetKeyDown(KeyCode.Return))
{
    ChangeColor(Color.green);
}
else if(Input.GetKeyDown(KeyCode.Space))
{
    ChangeColor(Color.blue);
}
}
```

Notice how we began the second `if` statement with the `else` keyword. We could have left it as a normal `if` statement and still achieved the same functionality, but using `else if` ensures that the second statement is only checked if the first one returns a false result. We'll never have a situation where we need to change the color twice in the same frame, so using `else` improves the efficiency of our code by handling either one case or the other.

8. Press the play button in the Unity editor and test your prototype to make sure the color of the text changes based on whether the *Return* key or the Space bar is pressed.

The *Return* key should still change the text to green, but the Space bar will turn the text to blue, as is shown in the following screenshot:

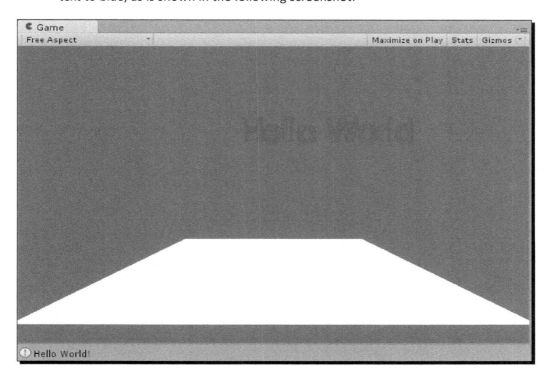

You've now created two different behaviors by calling the same function with two different parameters, but we're still not doing anything with the return value. To make sure we're successfully retrieving the position, we'll add a `print` statement to display it in the information bar at the bottom of the **Game** window.

9. Add the following `print` calls to each of your `ChangeColor` calls, as shown in the following code:

```
void Update()
{
   if(Input.GetKeyDown(KeyCode.Return))
   {
      print(ChangeColor(Color.green));
   }
   else if(Input.GetKeyDown(KeyCode.Space))
   {
      print(ChangeColor(Color.blue));
   }
}
```

The `print` function outputs whatever its parameters provide, which in our case is the return value from the `ChangeColor` function. Printing the return value is the simplest application of the returned data, but you can use it for anything, including assigning the value to a new variable, as shown in the following code:

```
Vector3 storedPosition = ChangeColor(Color.green);
```

10. Press the play button and change the color of the text with either the *Return* key or the Space bar to observe the printed returned position.

The `Vector3` position value will now be printed in the information bar in the bottom-left corner of the Unity editor, as shown in the following screenshot:

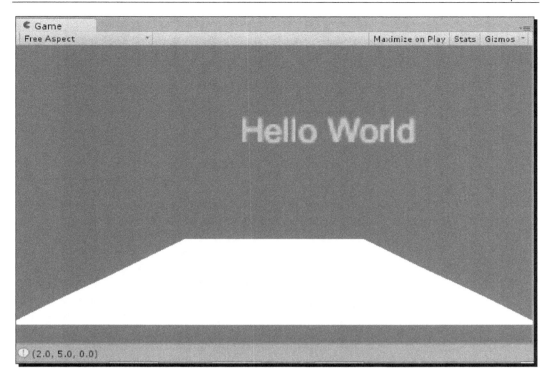

What just happened?

You've taken your first steps in creating interactive code by linking key presses to function calls in your Update function. You made the function dynamic by passing in a color as a parameter instead of explicitly defining it in code, and you returned position data of the calling object using the function's return value.

Input programming gets much more complex than the steps we've reviewed in this tutorial; input can do a lot more than just call a single function, and more complex statements are needed to check input from the OUYA controller instead of just a keyboard. However, before we dive into advanced controller input in the next chapter, we'll deploy what we have to the OUYA to make sure what we have so far is running (even though we can't control it on the OUYA without a keyboard attached to the console).

Deploying our code on OUYA

Now that you have something substantial to show, we'll deploy it to the OUYA and see how the scene carries over to the console.

Time for action – running your first test on OUYA

Perform the following steps to run your code on OUYA:

1. Verify that your project settings are properly configured for deploying to the OUYA.

2. Turn on your OUYA console and connect it to your computer with a USB cable.

3. Verify that your computer recognizes the OUYA console by using the following command in your command line:

   `adb devices`

> If your computer isn't able to locate the OUYA console immediately, the solution may be as simple as jump-starting the adb process. Run `adb kill-server` and then `adb devices` in your command line to restart the device manager and output a new list of connected devices.

4. Click on **Build & Run** in Unity's **File** menu to deploy your prototype to the console. As soon as it's finished building, your 3D text prototype will appear on the screen that your console is connected to.

Remember that you haven't coded any controller-based input yet, so your OUYA controller can't interact with the prototype, but if you connect your keyboard to one of the OUYA's USB ports, you can change the text color just like you could in the Unity editor.

> Just because you're programming for a console doesn't mean you can't use keyboard input like you've used in this chapter. Controller support is a must for all OUYA titles, but keyboard and mouse input is supported, and even encouraged, for complex games that native keyboard-and-mouse gamers may feel more comfortable with if they're using their preferred peripherals.

What just happened?

It's not a game yet, but deploying your 3D text prototype to the OUYA console is a good exercise in testing on the device itself; it is an important step in development. The more often you test on the console instead of in the editor, the more often you're experiencing exactly what players will see when they're playing your released product.

Keep in mind that there is no information bar to print values to when running your game on the OUYA. So, for testing that requires a lot of debugging and value reading (or several consecutive tests without spending too much time building and rebuilding), testing in the Unity editor may still be preferential.

Pop quiz – hello world

Q1. What can you use to conveniently store resultant data from a function call?

1. Function parameters
2. A return value
3. A local variable

Q2. What can you use to influence the values that a function interacts with?

1. Function parameters
2. A return value
3. A local variable

Q3. What's the name of the built-in Unity function that gets called with every frame?

1. `Start`
2. `Update`
3. `MoveObject`

Summary

You should now have a good understanding of how objects in Unity work. Many objects in your scene share common components such as positions and renderers, but the components of an object, including the scripts you create and attach, are what make it unique.

There is no shortage of pre-built objects, such as lights and cameras, in Unity. Some of these are vital to any game. Stock geometrical objects in Unity, such as planes, cubes, and spheres, are good for establishing basic shapes.

You've also learned all the programming fundamentals you'll need to make a game. It may seem like the code you wrote was small—and there is still plenty to learn—but knowing the anatomy of code as well as how to take advantage of every line and function keyword is the hardest part of programming; the fun lies in transforming your imagination into code.

In the next chapter, you'll continue working with scripts and write code that enables you to interact with the game objects in your scene using your keyboard and OUYA controller. Your knowledge of general input in Unity will form the foundation for all the game mechanics and prototypes you'll make over the course of this book.

4
Moving Your Player with Controller Input

One of the most important features of a well-developed game is a system that allows the player to move their character in a way that feels natural and intuitive. In the previous chapter, you wrote your first scripts to make objects move and change color based on a key press. In this chapter, you'll use the key press logic from the previous chapter to create an input script that moves the player in the game world. There's not one single right answer for how to process input and movement in your game, but in this chapter, we'll work with several techniques that contribute to a quality-control scheme. These techniques will be integrated into a "rolling marble" game prototype, which will give you the opportunity to learn about win and loss states.

In this chapter, we will cover the following topics:

◆ Creating an interactive marble prototype
◆ Adding additional functionalities to our marble
◆ Completing our game

Creating an interactive marble prototype

Our prototype will feature a marble that the player can move with the OUYA controller, a platform for the marble to roll around on. The prototype will also contain several coins for the player to collect by rolling into them. Input for the marble will be one of the first things we create, but before we do that, we have to set up the scene in our Unity project.

Time for action – setting the scene

To begin with, we'll use the basic scene elements from *Chapter 3, Diving into Development*, to quickly create a stage to start developing our game on. Perform the following steps to set the scene:

1. Open a new project in Unity and name it `RollingMarble`.

2. Create a directional light to illuminate the scene and set its position to 0, 0, 0.

    You may recall that the position of directional lights doesn't matter, but keeping things at the origin point of the scene makes it easy to find them when they've been highlighted.

     In two-dimensional coordinate systems, the value of 0 is sometimes used as a low-end boundary or the bottommost value. However, most 3D engines use 0 as the very center of the game world, instead of as an outlier. If you set an object's X, Y, and Z coordinates to 0, 0, and 0, its pivot point will be in the exact center of your scene.

3. After adding the light, add a cube from the **Create** menu in your **Hierarchy** menu. This cube can be used as the first platform for our marble to roll on.

    We used a plane as a surface in our last project, but planes have no depth and are only visible from the front face. We'll be able to build a more solid level with cubes of different sizes.

4. Position the cube at the origin point by setting its three position values to 0.

    The default cube is small and doesn't really look like a suitable platform to roll a marble on, so we'll alter its scale to make it more like a floor.

    Take a look at the tools panel in the upper-left corner of the Unity editor. So far, we've only been using the **Translate** tool to reposition objects, but we can use the other three tools (**Grab, Translate, Rotate**, and **Scale**) to interact with our scene and the objects within it in different ways.

    All of the object interaction tools are shown as icons in the Unity editor with inverse coloring on the currently selected tool, as shown in the following screenshot:

The four different tools, from left to right, are the Grab, Translate, Rotate, and Scale tools. The Grab tool affects your view of the entire scene, and the other three tools are all used for editing the properties of an object (which can also all be changed in the **Inspector** menu). You can see the differences between them in the following table:

Tool name/symbol	Purpose
Grab tool Symbol: hand	The Grab tool lets you grab your entire scene view and move it with the mouse as an alternative to navigating your scene with keyboard controls. This tool is good when you need to move your view very precisely.
Translate tool Symbol: four opposite arrows	The Translate tool, which we've used a little already, can be selected to move an object along the *x*, *y*, and *z* axes.
Rotate tool Symbol: two curved arrows	By selecting the Rotate tool, you can click-and-drag to rotate an object in any direction with a spherical rotating orb. Like the Translate tool, you can drag an individual axis or all three axes at once.
Scale tool Symbol: four arrows with a square	With the Scale tool, you can adjust the size of any object along an individual axis, or the universal size of the object by clicking-and-dragging from the middle; think of it as physically stretching the object.

 You can quickly switch between the four tools mentioned in the preceding table with the *Q*, *W*, *E*, and *R* keys. Each of them toggles the Grab, Translate, Rotate, and Scale tools, respectively.

5. Left-click on the Scale tool to activate it and then select your cube. Left-click and drag the *x* and *z* axes to make the cube into a broader platform.

   You can also reduce the **Y** scale to 0.5, because we don't need the floor to be extremely thick.

6. Exact numbers aren't necessary in this case, but ensure that your platform still lies around the origin point of the scene (0, 0, 0) and that your **X** and **Z** scale values are around 10. Your **Y** value should be around 0.5.

If you want it to be exact, remember to round off the values in the **Inspector** menu. Your scaled starting platform should look something like what is shown in the following screenshot:

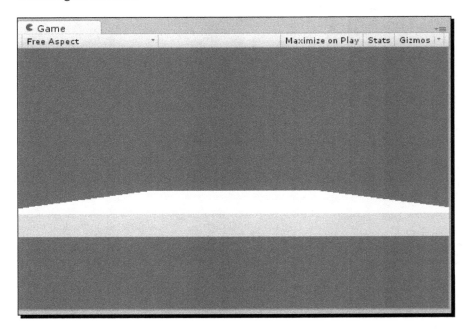

Now we'll create the marble that will roll around according to the player's input.

7. Create a new sphere from the **Create** menu in your **Hierarchy** menu and use the Translate tool to position it in the middle above the platform.

8. As we set the platform's position to 0 across all axes, we can zero out the sphere's X and Z coordinates to center the sphere on the platform and then drag the *y* axis until the sphere is slightly above the platform.

An exact elevation of the marble doesn't really matter, because once the marble is complete, Unity's built-in gravity will cause it to fall and hit the platform.

By this logic, you may be wondering why the platform that the marble falls on doesn't fall as well; after all, it's also loosely positioned in midair with no physical support to speak of. As it turns out, an object only responds to gravity if we tell it to by adding a rigidbody component to the object.

Adding a rigidbody to an object tells Unity that we want it to be a dynamic, movable force in our game world, affected by any external force that is applied to it. These forces include gravity, collision from other objects, and wind.

9. Add a rigidbody component to your sphere by highlighting it and clicking on **Add Component** in the **Inspector** menu.

10. Select the **Physics** submenu from the drop-down list and click on **Rigidbody**.

The new component should now appear in the list of components attached to the object in the **Inspector** window.

11. Press the play button and watch as the marble falls from its starting position until it lands on the platform.

The marble, with an attached rigidbody component, should look like what is shown in the following screenshot, in its resting position:

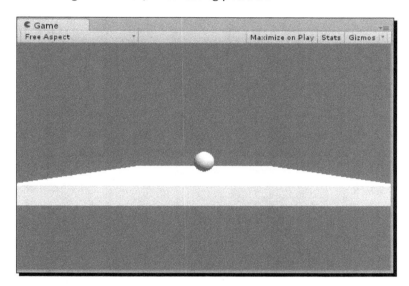

By adding a rigidbody component to the default sphere, we've turned a generic primitive into a unique object that's starting to suit our purpose for it. The more components you add to an object, the more dynamic and powerful it becomes. However, recreating an object with several components in another scene or in a different place within the same scene can be difficult and time consuming. For this, we have prefabs.

 A **prefab** (short for prefabrication) is like a blueprint for an object that you've created and/or modified. It stores all the components of a designated object and enables you to simply click-and-drag a new instance of that object onto your scene.

Let's create a prefab for our marble so that we can recreate it without having to make a sphere and then manually add the rigidbody component to it. It's worthwhile to create a separate folder for prefabs in your `Assets` directory, because you'll be using them a lot, and you're likely to have a lot of them when you start making bigger games.

> Folders can be created in the Unity editor or in your operating system's file explorer; creating it once using either method makes it accessible from anywhere. Note that Unity won't recognize new folders added outside of the editor until you click on it once again to make it the active window.

Right-click on your new folder after creating it, mouse over the **Create** menu, select **Prefab**, and name the prefab `Marble`.

You should see your prefab in your `Prefabs` folder accompanied by a gray cube icon, as shown in the following screenshot:

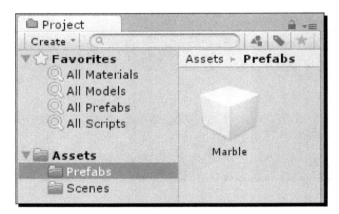

This gray cube icon means that the prefab hasn't been linked to any object's components yet.

12. Left-click and drag the sphere from your **Hierarchy** menu and release it over the `Marble` prefab.

The gray cube icon will become a preview icon, indicating that you've successfully stored the object in its current state in the prefab, and the object name in the **Hierarchy** menu will also turn blue to indicate that it's a product of a prefab. In the future, you can also create new prefabs simply by clicking-and-dragging the object from the scene into your `Prefabs` folder in the **Project** window.

You can still make changes to individual objects that were created from prefabs. Small changes such as variable values will even keep it linked with the prefab. However, if you make a large fundamental change to the object, such as removing a component, Unity will warn you that the operation will break the prefab connection. An object that breaks the prefab connection will retain all the components that it inherited from the prefab, but it will no longer update with the prefab or any other sibling objects that maintain a link with it.

What just happened?

At this point, you're probably warming up to Unity and getting used to the necessities and good practices for every scene you make. You've also learned how to create prefabs, which can be used to store all the components of an object into a blueprint that can then be used to create that same object without reattaching each component individually. The newest component that we've touched upon is the rigidbody component, which enables any object that is attached to it to respond to external forces such as gravity and collision. We were able to see this in real time by positioning a marble object with a rigidbody component above a platform and watching it fall. Next, we'll start coding some input so that we can control how the marble rolls. Remember to save the progress you've made, if you haven't done so, before you move on.

Time for action – importing a Unity input script

The Unity API has values that we can read in a script to tell whether the buttons on a controller are being pressed down. If you were to just use the core OUYA package for Unity, you would have to program your own input manager to act based on those values, but for the purposes of getting the game up and running quickly, you can import an existing script into your game from the OUYA community.

There are several viable input systems that we could find on the Internet, but in this tutorial, we'll use the **OuyaInput** controller framework by Matthias Titze. Navigate to the GitHub page for the open source project at `https://github.com/rendermat/OuyaInputFramework` and click on the **Download ZIP** button to download the files you'll need. When the zipped folder downloads, unzip it and open it to view the contents.

Now that you've acquired all of the necessary files for integrating input into your game, you can put the files into your Unity project by performing the following steps:

1. Move the `InputManager.asset` file from the downloaded folder to the `ProjectSettings` folder in your `Unity` project directory to replace the one that's included by default. This ensures that the axes' definitions are consistent with the input code.

2. Next, move the `OuyaInput.cs` script into your `Plugins` folder in the `Assets` directory. You won't have to write code in this script; it will just provide access to the input framework that we can access in our own scripts.

What just happened?

Installing the input library was as simple as downloading the files from the Web and dragging the `OuyaInput.cs` script into our `Plugins` folder. We also replaced the `InputManager.asset` file with a custom definition so that the input system would be able to access the correct controller mappings, but most plugins don't require you to edit files in the `ProjectSettings` directory.

Time for action – turning input into movement

We'll now use the input library you imported to capture data from the controller and translate it into movement that will be applied to our marble by performing the following steps:

1. Create a `Scripts` folder in your `Assets` directory to store all of your script files, if you haven't already done so, then right-click on it and create a new C# script.

2. Name the file `MarbleInputManager` and open it in your preferred code editor.

    Recall the `Start` and `Update` functions from *Chapter 3*, *Diving into Development*, which will already be present in the code file; we'll be using `Update` for most of this chapter.

3. To link the code file with your marble, left-click and drag it onto the prefab you created or add it as a new script component using the **Add Component** button in the **Inspector** menu.

    You can also drag it onto the actual marble on the screen, but this will only apply the script to that instance of the prefab; adding the script to the prefab itself will cause all the existing and future instances of that prefab to inherit the script.

4. Create two variables at the beginning of the script within the class definition: one called `moveVector` and one called `speed`. The `moveVector` variable will have a type of `Vector3` and the `speed` variable will be of type `float`.

5. Declare your variables and initialize the `speed` variable with a value of `500`, as shown in the following code:

```
Vector3 moveVector;
float speed;

void Start ()
{
  speed = 500.0f;
}
```

We'll use the `speed` variable to control how fast the marble responds to movement, and the `moveVector` variable will hold the direction that the marble should move in.

> `Vector3` is a data type we haven't worked with yet, but it's relatively simple—while types such as `float` hold a single number, `Vector3` variables hold three numbers for situations that demand more than one value, such as position (X, Y, and Z). Since we'll be applying the `moveVector` variable to the marble's position, it makes sense to store all three coordinate coefficients in a `Vector3` variable, instead of declaring three different `float` variables for it. Other variable types exist for vectors that hold a different number of values; `Vector2` holds two values and `Vector4` holds four.

Now we'll add code to the `Update` function to capture input from the user. Eventually, we'll expand our code to capture input specifically from the OUYA controller. However, first, we'll want the code that can also be tested with the keyboard in-editor, because it takes much less time than deploying for OUYA every time you want to test a change.

6. Put the following code in your empty `Update` function:

```
void Update ()
{
  moveVector.x = -Input.acceleration.y +
    Input.GetAxis("Horizontal");
  moveVector.z = -Input.acceleration.x +
    Input.GetAxis("Vertical");

  rigidbody.AddForce(moveVector * speed * Time.deltaTime);
}
```

Even though the preceding code is only three lines long, a lot happens in it so let's take a minute to step through it.

The first two lines are value assignments, denoted by the equal sign. We are setting the x and z values of our movement vector. These values which will be the axes that the marble moves across (the marble won't be moving up, so we don't need to set the y value). The numbers we assign to these values are calculated with some simple addition. We start with the last-measured acceleration of the input to account for any speed that the marble may have already accumulated in a certain direction.

We also access Unity's `Input` class, which isn't something you wrote a script for—`Input` is code that is built into Unity, and you can access it from any script to get information stored within the game engine, such as input data.

You may have noticed that we made the acceleration values negative and that the axis letters don't match. The axes of the `acceleration` variable don't match the orientation of our global position axes, so we had to use values that would still appear to move the marble in the direction of the arrow key.

After the acceleration value, we add the numerical return value of a Unity function called `GetAxis`. This function processes positive or negative input along a predefined axis, so we don't have to write conditional statements for all four directions. The input parameter for the `GetAxis` function is merely a `string` value that matches the name of the input axis. `Horizontal` and `Vertical` are already mapped to the arrow keys, so we didn't have to define them.

> Your options for capturing input with Unity's built-in input system aren't confined to any predefined values. By navigating to **Edit | Project Settings | Input**, you can view/edit all axes and input names, as well as add new ones. You'll notice that certain input axes have multiple entries, such as `Horizontal` and `Vertical`—this usually means that one entry is for capturing keyboard input and one is for capturing joystick input. If you still want to use them after they are overwritten by OUYA packages, just create new entries with the same values that they had before you imported them.

The last line of the `Update` function calls the `AddForce` function that all rigidbodies have and applies force on our marble along our directional vector at our speed. The last value in the multiplication, `Time.deltaTime`, is a Unity function common among many 3D game engines that ensures consistent movement. Since `Update` runs for every frame, our movement could be affected by lag and lost frames, but multiplying by `deltaTime`—a variable that keeps track of how much time has passed since the last frame—leaves the movement calculation unaffected by loss of frames.

What just happened?

Your game world moves by your command! We just scratched the surface of the capabilities of Unity's input system in this tutorial, but we covered the basics by capturing input along Unity's default vertical/horizontal axis definitions. Our code will expand when we're ready to capture OUYA-specific input, but for now, it's served its purpose by getting you used to the way input works. We housed our input code in the Update function, because we want it to update for every frame (virtually constantly) for accuracy and smoothness of animation.

You were also introduced to Time.deltaTime in this chapter. It is a very important variable to keep movement smooth. Multiplying a value by Time.deltaTime turns frame-by-frame movement into timed movement, so lag and loss of frames will never cause jumps or unexpected bugs.

Time for action – movement with the OUYA SDK

Now that you've got a good grasp on Unity input, let's program some OUYA-specific code so that we can see how it feels on the console. To do this, we'll need to import the OUYA input settings, which is part of the OUYA Core Package that we extracted in *Chapter 2, Installing Unity and the OUYA ODK*. Locate this package or refer to the chapter to re-extract it and import it into your current project by double-clicking on it or importing it as a custom package in the **Assets** menu along the top toolbar.

 Take a moment to open your **Input** settings in the **Project Settings** submenu under **Edit** on the top toolbar. Expand the **Axes** list in the **Inspector** menu and observe how the defined inputs have changed since importing the OUYA SDK Core Package; now there are several more defined inputs for joysticks and separate input channels for up to four controllers at once.

Before we add in OUYA controls, we need to think about how we'll be testing the game. Once our Update function captures input from the OUYA controller, it won't necessarily accept keyboard controls to test in the editor anymore. Fortunately, there's a code flag we can use to let the compiler identify which device the code is being run on, and we can write conditionals so the game can decide which code to run in which case. Perform the following steps to control movement with the OUYA SDK:

1. Add the following code in your Update function (the if statement at the beginning as well as the endif after the variable assignments):

```
void Update ()
{
#if UNITY_STANDALONE_WIN || UNITY_STANDALONE_OSX ||
  UNITY_EDITOR
```

```
    moveVector.x = -Input.acceleration.y +
      Input.GetAxis("Horizontal");
    moveVector.z = -Input.acceleration.x +
      Input.GetAxis("Vertical);
#endif
    rigidbody.AddForce(moveVector * speed * Time.deltaTime);
}
```

The #if and #endif flags serve as a conditional container for the code in between; it will only run if the if condition is met. In this case, it will only run if the game is being run on a standalone Unity client on Mac or Windows, or in the Unity editor. If you deployed this to the OUYA, nothing will be assigned to the moveVector variable. However, if you add an else flag, you can write code that will only execute if the game is run on the OUYA.

2. Add the following lines to your Update function:

```
void Update ()
{
#if UNITY_STANDALONE_WIN || UNITY_STANDALONE_OSX ||
  UNITY_EDITOR
    moveVector.x = -Input.acceleration.y +
      Input.GetAxis("Horizontal");
    moveVector.z = -Input.acceleration.x +
      Input.GetAxis("Vertical);
#else
    //OUYA-specific code goes here
#endif
    rigidbody.AddForce(moveVector * speed * Time.deltaTime);
}
```

The #else flag is more general in that it doesn't require a specified condition; it just executes if the preceding if condition is not met. So, the code following #else will be executed when the game is run on OUYA or any other platform that isn't the Unity editor. This is where we'll put our OUYA controller code.

3. Add the following lines to your Update function to handle controller input:

```
void Update ()
{
#if UNITY_STANDALONE_WIN || UNITY_STANDALONE_OSX ||
  UNITY_EDITOR
    moveVector.x = -Input.acceleration.y +
      Input.GetAxis("Horizontal");
    moveVector.z = -Input.acceleration.x +
      Input.GetAxis("Vertical);
#else
    //OUYA-specific code goes here
    moveVector.x = -Input.acceleration.y +
      OuyaInput.GetAxis(OuyaAxis.LX, OuyaPlayer.P01);
```

```
    moveVector.z = -Input.acceleration.x +
        OuyaInput.GetAxis(OuyaAxis.LY, OuyaPlayer.P01);
#endif
    rigidbody.AddForce(moveVector * speed * Time.deltaTime);
}
```

> If you're creating a project with multiple platforms and want to explicitly specify an OUYA/Android project, extend the #else flag to read #else if UNITY_ANDROID. If you want to write code for the OUYA but ignore all other Android platforms, add a normal line of code directly after the #else flag that reads #if(!OuyaSDK.IsOUYA()) return;.

The lines we added for the OUYA look a little more complex than the normal input code, but it's basically doing the same thing; it's just getting the axis value for the multiplication from the OUYA controller instead of the arrow keys.

What just happened?

Your code is now more dynamic and can handle input from both the OUYA controller and the keyboard, depending on what you deploy the game to. If you want to test your controller code, review the instructions for OUYA configuration in *Chapter 2, Installing Unity and the OUYA ODK*, and then click on **Build & Run** in Unity's **File** menu.

Next, we'll write code to make the marble hop. This can be triggered by the face buttons on the right-hand side of the OUYA controller. We'll also keep writing conditional statements that let us test using a keyboard and PC, as it's a good practice to handle multiple conditions, and it will let us test on whatever is more convenient.

Adding additional functionality to our marble

Let's give the marble a jumping ability so that the player can leap over obstacles. This will be pretty simple, but button input works a little differently than axis input, as you'll see in this section.

Movement code works well in the Update function, because it updates very slightly for every frame based on the position of the arrow keys or joysticks. However, jumping isn't a gradual movement; it's an immediate command. So, if we were to send a jump command while a button was pressed down, several frames would pass in the time that it took us to press the button and release it, resulting in several jumps sent in quick succession. To remedy this, we'll tell Unity to only send the jump command if the jump button is pressed down and was not pressed down in the last frame. This is done with an input function called GetKeyDown/ GetButtonDown. In the future, if you ever want to capture button status for every frame regardless of its earlier status, you will want to use the GetKey/GetButton function.

Time for action – adding button features

Kindly perform the following steps to add button features to our marble:

1. Add one new line each to the OUYA and non-OUYA code for applying a jump force to the rigidbody of our marble. The `Update` function will now look as follows:

```
void Update ()
{
#if UNITY_STANDALONE_WIN || UNITY_STANDALONE_OSX ||
  UNITY_EDITOR
  moveVector.x = -Input.acceleration.y +
    Input.GetAxis("Horizontal");
  moveVector.z = -Input.acceleration.x +
    Input.GetAxis("Vertical);

  if(Input.GetKeyDown(KeyCode.Space))
  {
    moveVector.y = 50.0f;
  }
  else
  {
    moveVector.y = 0.0f;
  }
#else
  //OUYA-specific code goes here
  moveVector.x = -Input.acceleration.y +
                    OuyaInput.GetAxis(OuyaAxis.LX,
                      OuyaPlayer.P01);
  moveVector.z = -Input.acceleration.x +
    OuyaInput.GetAxis(OuyaAxis.LY, OuyaPlayer.P01);

  if(Input.GetButtonDown("Jump"))
    moveVector.y = 50.0f;
  else
    moveVector.y = 0.0f;
#endif
  rigidbody.AddForce(moveVector * speed * Time.deltaTime);
}
```

The non-OUYA code now checks to see whether the Space bar was just pressed. If it was, the code applies an upward jump force to our movement vector. The OUYA code checks Unity's input library for the `Jump` entry that is bound to the A button on the OUYA controller and was added when you imported the OUYA SDK.

Notice that we used an `if/else` conditional statement to reset the jump force to zero if the button wasn't just pressed, but it looks different than our other `if/else` in our code. This is because the `if` statement we used to check what device the code is being run on is a compiler directive that speaks directly with the said device, but the statement we used for jumping is a common format that only deals with the game and not with the device.

What just happened?

You've now dealt with the two different types of input: axis input and button input. You know how to handle both of them on the OUYA and on the in-game editor. It's always good to code for both instances so that you can test quickly in the Unity environment without having to deploy to the OUYA just so that it can recognize your code.

To finish the chapter off, we'll extend our level to make it more like a path, add a win zone at the end, and have Unity load a "win screen" level once the player reaches it. However, before we do this, we should add a little more functionality to our main camera.

Time for action – improving the camera

Right now, our camera always stays in the same place. This confines our game to a very small area. To extend this area a little bit, we'll use one simple line of code that will keep the camera trained on our marble constantly. Perform the following steps to expand the viewing area of the camera:

1. Create a new C# script called `TrackingCamera` in your `Scripts` folder and open it up.

2. Add the following variable to the script above the `Start` function:

   ```
   public GameObject objectToTrack;

   void Start ()
   {

   }
   ```

   The `public` keyword before the `GameObject` variable type makes the variable accessible to the Unity editor and other scripts. We'll use this accessibility to our advantage and tell the script to track the marble right in the editor without any additional code.

3. Save the script and left-click and drag it onto the **Main Camera** object in your **Hierarchy** menu.

   In the new script pane on the camera's list of components, a slot for your public variable will appear just below the name of the script.

4. Click-and-drag the marble object from your **Hierarchy** menu onto the variable slot.

The slot in the **Inspector** window will appear, and it will look like the following screenshot:

This relationship can also be established in code without having to use the Unity editor, which we'll do in later chapters, but this simple technique will be sufficient for now. All we have to do to complete the camera's functionality is add a single line to the tracking script's Update function.

5. Add the following line to the Update function:

```
void Update ()
{
   transform.LookAt(objectToTrack.transform.position);
}
```

This Unity function will align the caller's rotation to look directly at a provided object. The camera won't change its position; it will only rotate, but even this will give us a larger amount of space to work with.

What just happened?

Sometimes, things are just easy. By writing two lines of code, you vastly expanded the viewing range of the main camera of the game with a built-in Unity function that makes it constantly look at a given object. It was even easy setting the object to track, by declaring the variable as public and dragging a valid object onto its slot in the Unity inspector.

Have a go hero – creating your own camera

The camera we just created will suit our needs for this chapter, but with the information you've learned over the last few chapters, you should be able to create a more robust camera that does even more. Here are some things to test out and try to implement in a new camera script:

◆ Make the camera move based on keyboard and controller input

◆ Implement manual rotation rather than automatic look-at rotation

◆ Enable the camera to zoom in and out (hint: use the z axis)

To implement manual rotation, you'll want to use the `Input` class that we've been using in combination with Unity's `transform.Rotate` function.

Completing our game

Every game needs an objective to reach or a goal to complete. Now that we've established a way for the player to move through the game world, we can add in a goal zone that triggers a victory state when the player touches it.

Time for action – adding a goal zone

Perform the following steps to add a goal zone and complete our game:

1. Extend your main platform by adding other platforms that create a straight path.

2. Reposition your marble to start on the leftmost platform so that it can be rolled to the rightmost one.

   Exact positioning isn't necessary; just make sure your marble can roll from one platform to another.

3. Add in at least one small wall for your marble to jump over in order to reach the end.

   Your finished product should look somewhat similar to the following screenshot:

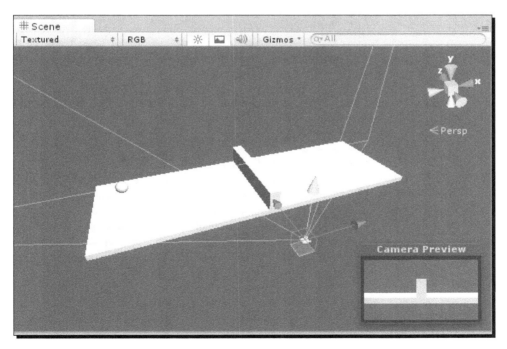

Next, we'll create the goal object by performing the following steps:

4. Create a new cube with default scale and put it somewhere on the other side of the wall.

We will want to know when our marble hits the goal, so we'll write a code to access the collider property of this goal object.

5. Create a new C# script called `GoalBox`, attach it to your new cube, and open it for editing.

Just like the rigidbody component, the collider component also grants the parent object access to some specific functionality. One such function for the collider component is the `OnCollisionEnter` function, which can be extended by creating a definition for it in a script.

6. Add the `OnCollisionEnter` function to the `GoalBox` script with a collider parameter, as shown in the following code:

```
void Update()
{

}

void OnCollisionEnter(Collision obj)
{

}
```

We'll eventually add code to this function that will take us to a win screen, but first, we need a win screen.

7. Save this scene as `level1` and create a new scene in your `Scenes` folder called `WinScreen`.

We won't need to spend much time here; at this point, our win screen's only purpose is to notify us that we've reached the end. Add a new 3D text object that says **You Win!** and position it in the center of the camera's view, as shown in the following screenshot:

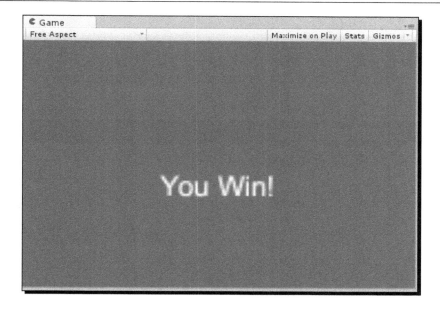

Now, all we need to do is add both scenes to the list of scenes in the build so that the application can recognize both scenes and switch from one to the other.

8. Navigate to **File | Build Settings...** and click on **Add Current**.

9. Save the win screen scene, open the scene in which your first level is, and add it with the **Add Current** button.

Now that both scenes are recognized by the build, we just need to add code that displays the win screen when the player reaches the goal.

10. Return to your OnCollisionEnter function and add the following code:

```
void OnCollisionEnter(Collider obj)
{
    Application.LoadLevel("WinScreen");
}
```

11. Save changes to the script, double-check to make sure you've added it as a component to your goal cube, and press play.

Use the input commands you programmed to move the marble to the goal box, and as soon as you hit it, your win screen will be displayed. You've done it!

What just happened?

Give yourself a pat on the back; you made a small game, but you made a game nonetheless. Player input and win/loss states are fundamental to any game, and it is great to know about the `Application.LoadLevel` function to switch between multiple scenes or levels in a Unity game.

Pop quiz – coming full circle

Q1. Which of the following lines could be used to restart the game when the player presses the Space bar?

1. ```
   if(Input.GetKeyDown(KeyCode.Space))
       Application.LoadLevel("SceneOne");
   ```

2. ```
   if(OuyaSDK.IsOUYA()) Application.LoadLevel("SceneOne");
   ```

3. ```
   if(Input.GetKeyDown(Input.Space))
       Application.LoadLevel("SceneOne");
   ```

Q2. How can you add a component to an object in the scene without affecting the prefab that it's connected to?

1. Add the component to the prefab using the **Inspector** menu

2. Add the component to the object in the **Hierarchy** menu

3. Recreate the object using primitives

Summary

In this chapter, you created your first actual game. You programmed input code that the player can use to control their "character" (a marble, in this case) and added a goal zone that brings your player to the win screen as soon as they reach it. All of the code you've written so far has been pretty basic, but now that we've covered the fundamentals, we'll start delving into the more complex parts of what makes games fun and unique.

In the next chapter, you'll build your skills even further by turning simple game prototypes into advanced fun mechanics with the help of the OUYA controller's unique touch panel.
   ```

5
Enhancing Your Game with Touch Dynamics

In the previous chapter, Chapter 4, Moving Your Player with Controller Input, you learned how to capture basic input from the player and enable them to navigate the game world with both the keyboard and the OUYA controller. Methods of processing input as well as everything else you've learned in this book so far are techniques that aren't just applicable to OUYA games; game logic such as player input and cameras are present in every game, and Unity projects can be deployed to many more platforms other than Android, such as iOS, Windows, OS X, and BlackBerry. However, certain features exist exclusively in the OUYA API that you can program to make full use of the console, as you'll discover in this chapter.

One of the OUYA's unique features is the touchpad on all OUYA controllers. By default, the touchpad functions as a basic mouse cursor that can be moved around the screen by dragging a finger across the touchpad surface. This is available automatically in any OUYA game even if you don't program it, but you can add scripts to your game that override this function and use the touch data to add special mechanics to your game.

In this chapter, we'll cover the following topics:

◆ Using the touchpad to interact with buttons
◆ Using cursor data to add touch input to games
◆ Incorporating touch data into your mechanics

Using the touchpad to interact with buttons

To get a good feel of how the OUYA touchpad works, we'll begin by utilizing its most simple functionality: clicking on the GUI buttons. We'll create and expand on a cannonball game prototype throughout the chapter, creating a clickable button to fire a cannonball and eventually overriding the touch functionality to calculate the power and angle based on a swipe gesture.

Creating the cannonball prototype

The goal of our cannonball game will be to hit a target on the other side of the screen by applying a variable force to the cannon prefab. Before we implement touch functionality, we have to create the cannon itself.

Time for action – creating a cannon prefab

Perform the following steps to create a cannon prefab:

1. Create a new Unity project titled `TouchCannon`.

   You're probably used to setting up scenes at this point, so we'll start by quickly establishing the base elements we need.

2. Import your OUYA Core package into the Unity scene.

3. Set the project to Android from a standalone, and make sure your player settings match the settings we went over in *Chapter 2, Installing Unity and the OUYA ODK*. We need to actually deploy to the OUYA to test this prototype because it relies on the OUYA controller's touchpad.

4. Create a new plane positioned at 0, 0, 0 and increase its **X** scale to 10 because we want the cannon and target to be on opposite ends of a horizontal platform.

5. Create a directional light with default settings—you may recall that positions of directional lights is irrelevant, so you can put it wherever you like.

6. Finally, position the main camera at 0, 10, -25 so that the entire platform is in view from above.

After you've done all of this, your game screen should look similar to the following screenshot:

7. Now's a good time to save your scene. Create a `Scenes` folder in your `Assets` directory and save this scene as `game.unity`.

Next, we'll create the cannon prefab that we'll eventually code to receive the touch input. So far, we've only used primitive objects in our prototypes, but we want this prefab to be a discernible cannon, so we'll combine some basic shapes and link them all together to make a more complex model.

8. Start by creating a basic cube that will serve as the root object. As it's the center of the cannon, scale it up to twice its original size to make sure it isn't too small.

9. Next, create a basic cylinder and use the Move tool to position it within the cube, pointing out at an angle, as shown in the following screenshot:

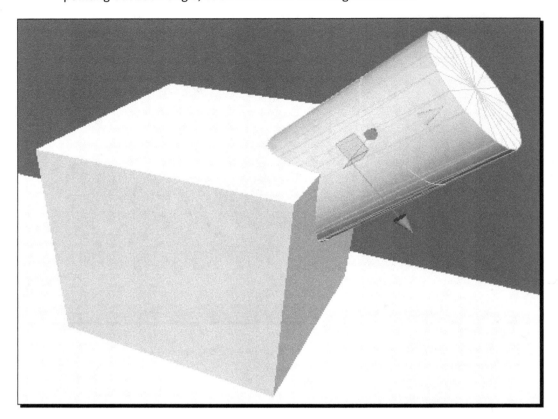

10. Once you're happy with the position of the cylinder, find it in the **Hierarchy** window, hold left-click over it, and drag it onto the root cube in the hierarchy.

When you release the left-mouse button, the cylinder will become a child of the root cube, which means the cylinder position, movement, and rotation are locked to that cube. You've effectively combined the cylinder and the cube to be a single object, using the cube as a root.

Here's a chance to let your artistic side shine; you can link any number of primitive shapes to the root cube to make your cannon look exactly how you want, and as long as they're all added to the cube object in the hierarchy, they'll act as one.

11. Add some other objects to the cube to make the cannon look nice as the focus of your prototype.

When you turn your object into a prefab, all of your positioned objects will be saved, so you don't have to worry about adding meticulous details to your cannon more than once. After adding some basic shapes, your cannon will begin to take a clear form, as shown in the following screenshot:

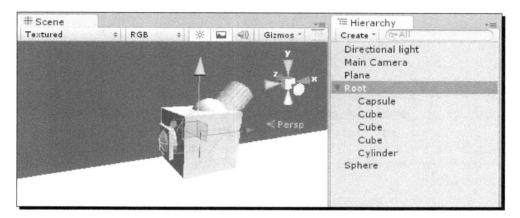

Obviously, models in final games aren't made of primitive shapes; 3D modeling software allows game artists to manipulate faces, vertices, and edges of complex meshes to create realistic and stylized game objects. While programming and prototyping, you won't need fancy models, but before publishing a game on the OUYA marketplace, you may consider taking up modeling or partnering up with a 3D artist to really make your game pop.

>
> If you want to get into 3D modeling but don't want to buy software just yet, check out Blender at blender.org. It's a free, open source modeling software that can export models that can be imported into Unity. The Blender community also offers several tutorials and resources for beginners.

The last step to finishing our cannon is to link it to a prefab.

12. Create a new folder called Prefabs in your Assets directory and right-click on it to access the **Create** menu.

13. Create a new prefab called Cannon and drag your cannon object from the hierarchy onto it to complete the prefab link.

The root object's name will turn blue in the hierarchy, and you'll now be able to create as many cannons as you want by dragging the Cannon prefab onto the scene. You can even delete the original object and create a fresh one from the prefab if you want.

14. Once you're finished, position your cannon at -20, 1, 0 so that it lies on the left-hand side of the platform in the game window.

What just happened?

You've added multiple scripts to prefabs in previous tutorials, and now you've added multiple physical objects as well. The more complex a prefab becomes, the more its value becomes apparent. Combining primitives in prefabs is a great way to get the game's tone across to anyone who sees it in an unfinished state, when you may be waiting on final 3D models or iterating visual styles. Whether you're demoing it for a friend or pitching it to a potential investor, a little bit of visual polish goes a long way, regardless of how good your code is.

Time for action – creating an interactive button

Now that you've created a cannon prefab, we can start writing scripts for it that use the OUYA controller's touchpad. The first functionality we'll add is an interactive button that makes the cannon fire a cannonball when it's tapped. Perform the following steps to add an interactive button:

1. Create a new script named `CannonScript.cs` in your `Code` folder and attach it to your `Cannon` prefab.

2. Open `CannonScript.cs` in your code editor.

3. Declare the following variables at the top of the `CannonScript` class definition, just before the `Start` function:

```
private int buttonWidth;
private int buttonHeight;
private string buttonText;

void Start()
{

}
```

4. Initialize each variable with values for our new button in the `Start` function. Give the button a width of `100`, a height of `50`, and a `"Fire!"` text label, as shown in the following code:

```
Private int buttonWidth;
private int buttonHeight;
private string buttonText;

Void Start()
{
```

```
    buttonWidth = 100;
    buttonHeight = 50;
    buttonText = "Fire!";
}
```

The button we're going to create will be a part of our **Graphical User Interface** (GUI), so we'll add a function definition to extend Unity's built-in OnGUI function. The OnGUI function is run for every frame, much like the Update function, but it is run specifically when Unity is rendering 2D user interface elements.

5.   Add OnGUI directly below your Update function, as shown in the following code:

```
void Update()
{

}

void OnGUI()
{

}
```

6.   Insert the following lines into the OnGUI function to display a button with your preset properties:

```
void OnGUI()
{
  if(GUI.Button(new Rect(Screen.width / 2 - buttonWidth /2, 0,
    buttonWidth, buttonHeight), buttonText))
  {
    //code to run when button is pressed goes here
  }
}
```

The GUI.Button function can create a default button with minimal parameters, requiring only a position, width, height, and text.

The first parameter of our button's rectangle, Screen.width / 2 - buttonWidth / 2, positions our button in the direct horizontal center of the screen. Screen.width / 2 produces a coordinate in the middle of the screen, and subtracting buttonWidth / 2 accounts for the offset of the button's upper-left anchor. The second parameter is the vertical position, which we left at 0, so it will appear to be at the very top of the screen.

> If you're having trouble seeing your GUI element on your TV but
> not in the Unity editor, it may be hidden by the TV's overscan. You
> can fix this by setting the Y value slightly higher, depending on how
> much overscan your TV has; try a value of 0.1 or 0.2. We'll get into
> the details of compensating for overscan in a later chapter.

7. Verify that your button is drawn correctly by pressing the play button in the
Unity editor.

Your button should be displayed in the top-center section of the screen, as shown in
the following screenshot:

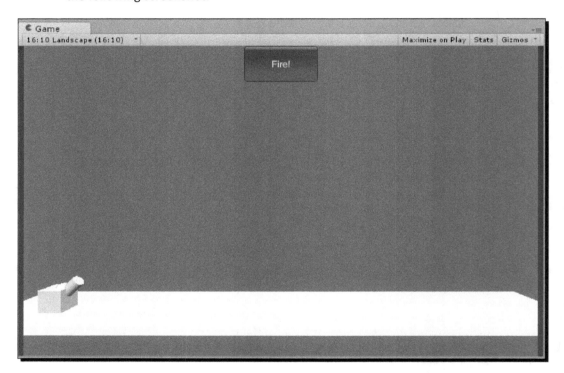

Now that the button is displayed properly, we can script code so that it can be run
whenever it's pressed. We want the cannon to fire a new cannonball every time the
code is called, so first, we'll need to create a cannonball prefab.

8. Create a new sphere from the **Create** menu in the **Hierarchy** window.

9. Create a new material called CannonballMat in your **Project** window, color it black
with a specular shader, and drag it on to the sphere to apply it.

Your sphere with the shiny black material applied should now look enough like a cannonball, as shown in the following screenshot:

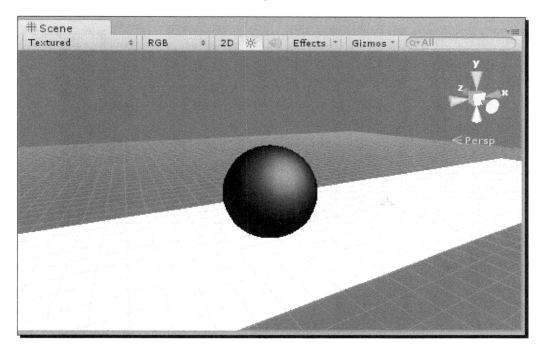

10. Create a new prefab called Cannonball in the Prefabs folder.

11. Link the sphere to your Cannonball prefab by clicking-and-dragging it from the **Hierarchy** window to the prefab in the **Project** window.

12. Delete the sphere you created as the base for the cannonball; we can create as many cannonballs as we want with our prefab, and there's no reason to have a cannonball hanging around in our scene.

   The only thing our cannonball needs now is a rigidbody component so that it can behave like a physical object.

13. Left-click on the Cannonball prefab in the **Project** window to display it in the **Inspector** menu.

14. Click on the **Add Component** button, select the **Physics** menu, and click on **Rigidbody** to add a rigidbody component to the Cannonball prefab.

   Our cannonball is complete, and we're ready to incorporate it into our script.

15. Declare a public `GameObject` variable called `cannonballPrefab` next to your other variables in the `CannonScript` class, as shown in the following code:

```
private int buttonWidth;
private int buttonHeight;
private string buttonText;
public GameObject cannonballPrefab;
```

16. Link the `Cannonball` prefab to the new variable by dragging the prefab onto the new public `CannonballPrefab` field in the cannon's **Inspector** window.

When the prefab has been properly linked, your `CannonScript` component should look like the following screenshot in the **Inspector** window:

The `cannonballPrefab` variable will allow our `CannonScript` code to create a new instance of the cannonball every time the button is pressed.

17. Create a new function called `FireCannon` in your `CannonScript` class:

```
void FireCannon()
{

}
```

18. Create a variable of type `Vector3` for the new cannonball's position and initialize it with the cannon's position as shown in the following code:

```
void FireCannon()
{
  Vector3 cannonballPos = gameObject.transform.position;
}
```

19. Offset the cannonball's position from the cannon's position by adjusting the x and y values as shown:

```
void FireCannon()
{
  Vector3 cannonballPos = gameObject.transform.position;
  cannonballPos.x += 2;
  cannonballPos.y += 2;
}
```

20. Add a line that instantiates a new cannonball at our newly created location:

```
void FireCannon()
{
  Vector3 cannonballPos = gameObject.transform.position;
  cannonballPos.x += 2;
  cannonballPos.y += 2;

  Instantiate(cannonballPrefab, cannonballPos,
    Quaternion.identity);
}
```

> The rotation argument for our call to `Instantiate`, which we set as `Quaternion.identity`, is basically the rotational equivalent of zero, or the object's default rotation. As we don't care how the object is rotated when it's instantiated (especially because the rotation doesn't affect the appearance or trajectory of spheres), using `Quaternion.identity` is fine for this instantiation.

21. Finally, add a call to your `FireCannon` function to your button statement in `OnGUI` as shown:

```
void OnGUI()
{
  if(GUI.Button(new Rect(Screen.width / 2 - buttonWidth / 2, 0,
    buttonWidth, buttonHeight), buttonText))
  {
    //code to run when button is pressed goes here
    FireCannon();
  }
}
```

Our cannon is now capable of firing cannonballs whenever the **Fire!** button is pressed.

22. Click on **Build & Run** in the **File** menu to deploy your prototype to the OUYA console.

23. Test your new firing functionality by moving the touch cursor over the new button and tapping it.

You'll notice that as we haven't coded a physical force on the cannonballs yet, they just fall out of the cannon when they're instantiated:

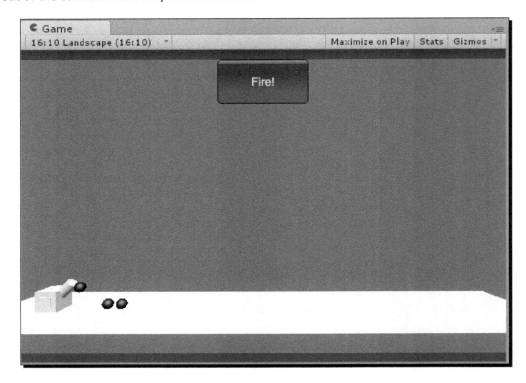

The next step will be to add a force to these cannonballs at the moment of instantiation so that we can make them really fly.

What just happened?

You just created a button that can instantiate a new cannonball at our cannon's location with a click or a touch. Unity interprets OUYA's default touchpad cursor in the same way that it interprets a mouse on a computer, so no additional coding was needed to make the button compatible with both the PC and the OUYA cursor inputs.

The OUYA touchpad cursor can be moved by dragging a finger across the touchpad on the controller, and a "click" is performed simply by tapping a finger on the face of the touchpad. This basic functionality is all built into Unity, but we'll push the touchpad's capabilities even further later on in the chapter when we add swipe gestures. Before we do that, however, we need to give our cannonballs some force.

Time for action – adding an impulse force to a rigidbody component

Force can be applied to any `GameObject` variable that has a `rigidbody` component using Unity's `AddForce` function. In the case of our cannonballs, we want to add force to them as soon as they're instantiated; so in this section, we'll be editing our `FireCannon` function to include an additional force on any new cannonballs.

To change the properties of an instantiated prefab, we need a variable linked to it. Fortunately, Unity's `Instantiate` function returns the instantiated prefab, so we can store that in a new local variable in our `FireCannon` function. Perform the following steps to add an impulse:

1. Modify the call to `Instantiate` in your `FireCannon` function to store the return value in a new `GameObject`:

```
void FireCannon()
{
  Vector3 cannonballPos = gameObject.transform.position;
  cannonballPos.x += 2;
  cannonballPos.y += 2;

  GameObject newCannonball =
    (GameObject)Instantiate(cannonballPrefab, cannonballPos,
      Quaternion.identity);
}
```

   Note that in addition to declaring a new `GameObject` variable, we also wrote `GameObject` in parentheses before the `Instantiate` function call. This is called **typecasting**, and essentially, it just tells the function what we're expecting to receive from it, even if that function doesn't explicitly return that type by default. A lot of function returns don't need to be typecasted, but `Instantiate` can return a lot of different general information that doesn't only apply to `GameObject` variables, so we explicitly typecasted the return as `GameObject` so that it can be manipulated like one. Now that we have a `GameObject` variable that points to our newly instantiated cannonball, we can manipulate its properties even after it's instantiated.

2. Add the following line to your `FireCannon` function to give the cannonball some initial force in the direction of the cannon's barrel:

```
void FireCannon()
{
  Vector3 cannonballPos = gameObject.transform.position;
  cannonballPos.x += 2;
  cannonballPos.y += 2;
```

```
GameObject newCannonball =
    (GameObject)Instantiate(cannonballPrefab, cannonballPos,
     Quaternion.identity);

newCannonball.rigidbody.AddForce(12.5f, 12.5f, 0f,
   ForceMode.Impulse);
}
```

There are several different parameter sets that can be passed into `AddForce` depending on what you're trying to do, but for our purposes, we used the one that takes three positional values and a `ForceMode` class. The first three values refer to the *x*, *y*, and *z* coordinate values, respectively, and `ForceMode` is a Unity class that lets you define how the force is applied. The four different `ForceMode` options are listed in the following table:

Options	Description
Force	This is the most basic `ForceMode` option. It is typically used when applying a continuous force such as a push or pull. Mass is considered in this equation.
Acceleration	Similar to `Force`, this adds a constant acceleration to an object, but it does not take the mass of the object into account. This would be used to simulate physics equations that don't rely on mass, such as Earth's gravitational pull.
Impulse	This adds an immediate force to an object over the course of one frame, taking the mass of the object into consideration. This is used in forces that represent an impact, such as an object being fired or an instantaneous motion.
VelocityCharge	This instantly adjusts the object's velocity without regarding mass. This can be used in the same cases as an impulse force where the mass of the object doesn't matter.

We used `Impulse` because a cannonball being fired from a cannon is most closely related to an instantaneous and powerful force that doesn't maintain itself after the initial impact.

3. Test your new code by starting the game and pressing the **Fire!** button again, either in the Unity editor or by deploying it to the OUYA.

You'll see that your cannonballs now fly horizontally across the scene whenever you click on the **Fire!** button, as shown in the following screenshot:

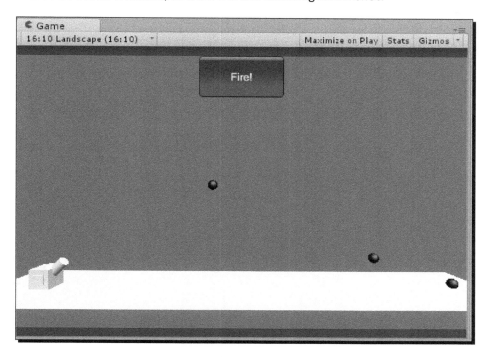

What just happened?

You've now integrated the basic touch functionality into your cannon's firing mechanic using the OUYA controller's touchpad or a mouse to call the FireCannon function. However, touch controls don't stop at buttons; clicking/tapping is only the most basic of several ways you can make your game more unique with non-standard controls.

Next, we'll explore another one of these techniques by writing code that collects the cursor's position over several frames and uses it to analyze gestures such as swiping.

Using cursor data to add touch input to games

Gesture touch controls have become increasingly popular with the presence of mobile touchscreen devices, and even though there aren't any gestures built in to the OUYA SDK, the idea behind them is simple enough that we can code a solution ourselves.

Essentially, every touch gesture has a start point, an end point, and a speed at which the player's finger moves between them. In this section, we'll create variables for this data and create a function that fires a cannonball with a speed and angle based on a touch gesture.

Time for action – reading mouse position in Unity

To begin, we'll create a GUI object that displays the *x* and *y* coordinates of our mouse as we move it. We'll be able to observe the range and current position of the mouse, which we can then use to write a gesture function. Perform the following steps to read mouse position:

1. Open the **Create** menu in the **Hierarchy** window and select **GUI Text** to create a new text object.

2. Your default **GUI Text** object will appear as shown in the following screenshot:

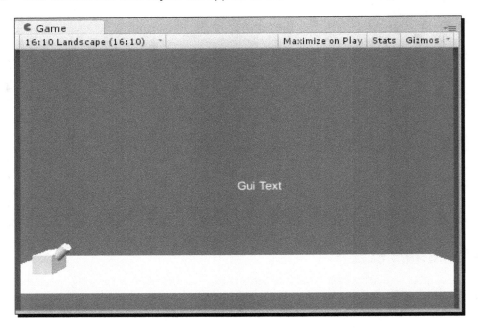

    We don't want this text to obscure our game at all, so we'll reposition it to stay in the upper-left corner of the screen.

3. Click on the **GUI Text** object in the **Hierarchy** window to display it in the **Inspector** window.

4. Change the **X** and **Y** values of the **GUI Text** object's **Transform** component to 0 and 1, respectively.

5. Change the color of the text in the object by selecting a new color from the **Color** field in the **GUIText** component.

After performing the previous two steps, your **GUI Text** object should appear as shown in the following screenshot in the **Inspector** window:

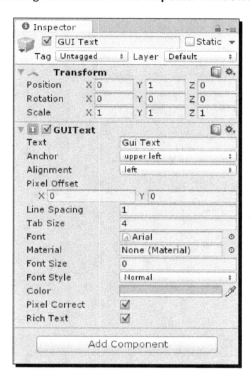

Next, we need to script the actual text to display on the object.

6. Create a new script called `MousePositionText.cs` and open it in your code editor.

7. Add the following line to the script's `Update` function:

```
void Update()
{
  gameObject.guiText.text = "X: " + Input.mousePosition.x + "
    Y: " + Input.mousePosition.y;
}
```

Wondering why we're using the addition operator (+) when coding the text to display? In the context of text, or strings, the addition operator can be used to link multiple pieces of text together from one end to another. Unity can convert many simple data types into a string value, so we can use the *x* and *y* coordinates of the mouse position as dynamic text and tie it all together using the addition operator.

8. Click on play in the Unity editor and move your mouse around the screen to see your mouse position text update.

The text will update every time the Update function is run (for every frame), and it will display your mouse position data as shown in the following screenshot:

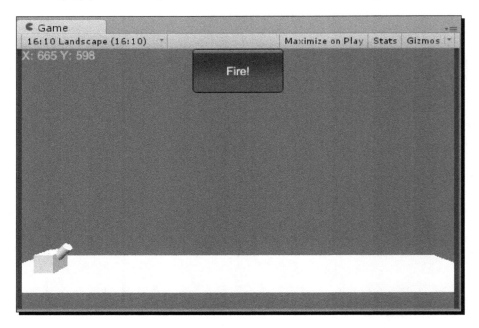

If you aren't testing the game in fullscreen, keep in mind that the mouse position data will reflect the position of your mouse on the monitor, not just inside the **Game** view. However, this is something we'll never have to consider in code because games are always displayed in fullscreen on the OUYA.

What just happened?

You've now created a dynamic text object that displays the coordinates of your cursor on the screen. We haven't done anything with that data yet, but it's always a good idea to create text to visualize the data before or during your implementation. This is commonly referred to as **debug text** because it helps programmers conceptualize and debug their mechanics, but is not included in the game's final interface.

Next, we'll start saving the values displayed into variables so that we can use them in our velocity and angle calculations.

Time for action – creating a vector from cursor movement

Our cannonballs are propelled by an initial force that we create using the X and Y elements of the AddForce vector. Up until this point, the two values were set at a constant value of 12.5, creating the same velocity and angle each time.

In this section, we'll use the change in the X and Y values from our cursor to affect the dynamic X and Y values in our firing function so that the velocity and angle are affected by the way the cursor is moved. Perform the following steps to create the vector:

1. Declare two new `float` variables called `mouseX` and `mouseY` next to the other variables in your `CannonScript.cs` file as shown:

```
private int buttonWidth;
private int buttonHeight;
private string buttonText;
public GameObject cannonballPrefab;

private float mouseX;
private float mouseY;
```

2. Create a new function called `CaptureTouch` in `CannonScript.cs` using the following code:

```
void CaptureTouch()
{

}
```

As swipe gestures happen over multiple frames of our game, we need to be able to capture the touch data for every frame.

3. Add a call to `CaptureTouch` in the `Update` function as shown in the following code:

```
void Update()
{
  CaptureTouch();
}
```

4. Add the following lines to `CaptureTouch` to store the cursor's x and y coordinates in your new variables:

```
void CaptureTouch()
{
  mouseX = Input.mousePosition.x;
  mouseY = Input.mousePosition.y;
}
```

As we need to capture cursor data for every frame, it would be inefficient to act on the data if it hasn't changed or isn't being used.

5. Add a statement that checks whether the mouse position has changed since the last frame and return from the function if it hasn't. Make sure that you keep the assignments to mouseX and mouseY at the very end of the function because we don't want to synchronize the values until we get the difference between them.

```
void CaptureTouch()
{
  if(mouseX == Input.mousePosition.x && mouseY ==
    Input.mousePosition.y)
    return;

  mouseX = Input.mousePosition.x;
  mouseY = Input.mousePosition.y;
}
```

 Writing a single-line statement in the body of a function that returns if certain conditions are met (or not met) is called an **early return**. Using this is a great way to give your processor some slack if the conditions recognize that the rest of the function is useless. Note that there are no curly braces enveloping the previous statement; for single-line statements, you can simply write the line to be run directly after the if statement. However, if you wanted to expand the conditional functionality to run multiple lines, you would need to insert brackets like we've done in our other conditional statements.

If the statement does not trigger a return, we can assume that the mouse is currently in motion. The next step is to measure the distance that the cursor has traveled by subtracting the current distance from the previous distance.

6. Create the following temporary variables inside your CaptureTouch function and initialize them as shown:

```
void CaptureTouch()
{
  if(mouseX == Input.mousePosition.x && mouseY ==
    Input.mousePosition.y)
    return;

  float deltaX = Input.mousePosition.x - mouseX;
  float deltaY = Input.mousePosition.y - mouseY;

  mouseX = Input.mousePosition.x;
  mouseY = Input.mousePosition.y;
}
```

The term **delta** refers to a value of change, so we named our new variables `deltaX` and `deltaY` to reflect the change in their respective coordinates. You may remember using a value called `Time.deltaTime` in *Chapter 4*, *Moving Your Player with Controller Input*; this is another value of change, representing the amount of time that has passed since the last frame.

We've got the changed values that we'll use to fire our cannon, but currently we don't have a firing function that takes any parameters. Create a new `FireCannon` function below your current `FireCannon` function that takes two `float` values as shown:

```
void FireCannon(float xForce, float yForce)
{

}
```

 Your code can contain multiple functions of the same name, but only if they have different parameters. This is called **function overloading**. You can use this to your advantage as a developer. By creating a function that can handle all different kinds of parameters, you enable that function to be called with one of many inputs without the need to typecast.

Define your new `FireCannon` function in the same way as your old one, but with the `xForce` and `yForce` variables taking the place of the `12.5` constant force value:

```
void FireCannon(float xForce, float yForce)
{
  Vector3 cannonballPos = gameObject.transform.position;
  cannonballPos.x += 2;
  cannonballPos.y += 2;

  GameObject newCannonball =
    (GameObject)Instantiate(cannonballPrefab, cannonballPos,
      Quaternion.identity);

  newCannonball.rigidbody.AddForce(xForce, yForce, 0f,
    ForceMode.Impulse);
}
```

Now add a line to your `CaptureTouch` function that calls `FireCannon` with the cursor delta values:

```
void CaptureTouch()
{
  ...

  float deltaX = Input.mousePosition.x - mouseX;
  float deltaY = Input.mousePosition.y - mouseY;
```

```
      FireCannon(deltaX, deltaY);

      mouseX = Input.mousePosition.x;
      mouseY = Input.mousePosition.y;
   }
```

Your code is almost ready to test, but we're missing one thing. Right now, FireCannon is called every time there's a change in mouse position, even if the change is part of the same swipe from a different frame. We don't want to instantiate multiple cannonballs on a single swipe, so we'll add a boolean value that ignores the CaptureTouch function if we're in the middle of a swipe.

7. Create a boolean variable called isSwiping next to your other variables and initialize it as false as shown in the following code:

```
...
private float mouseX;
private float mouseY;

private bool isSwiping = false;
```

8. Add another early return to your CaptureTouch function that exits if a swipe is being made:

```
void CaptureTouch()
{
   if(mouseX == Input.mousePosition.x && mouseY ==
     Input.mousePosition.y)
      return;

//exit the function if a swipe is being made
   if(isSwiping == true)
      return;
}
```

9. We need to mark the isSwiping variable as true every time a cannonball is being fired, so add a line that sets isSwiping to true if the cursor is moved while isSwiping is false:

```
Void CaptureTouch()
{
   ...
   //exit the function if a swipe is being made
   if(isSwiping == true)
   {
     mouseX = Input.mousePosition.x;
     mouseY = Input.mousePosition.y;
```

```
        return;
    }
    else
        isSwiping = true;
    ...
}
```

Note that we capture the cursor values even if a swipe is in progress because we still need to check their state in the next frame.

Finally, we need to set `isSwiping` to `false` if the mouse isn't moving, so add a line to your first early return that checks the change in the position. The following code is the full `CaptureTouch` function:

```
void CaptureTouch()
{
    if(mouseX == Input.mousePosition.x && mouseY == Input.
mousePosition.y)
    {
        isSwiping = false;
        return;
    }

    if(isSwiping == true)
    {
        mouseX = Input.mousePosition.x;
        mouseY = Input.mousePosition.y;
        return;
    }
    else
        isSwiping = true;
    float deltaX = Input.mousePosition.x - mouseX;
    float deltaY = Input.mousePosition.y - mouseY;

    FireCannon(deltaX, deltaY);

    mouseX = Input.mousePosition.x;
    mouseY = Input.mousePosition.y;
}
```

Your code is finally ready for testing and will instantiate and fire a cannonball every time the cursor is moved based on the direction of the movement.

10. Test your new mechanics by starting the game and moving the cursor.

You'll notice that the cannonballs don't have much force behind them anymore. That's because the cursor's delta values are captured for every frame, so the instantaneous change is much smaller than our original constant force value of `12.5`. To remedy this, we'll multiply the delta values in the `AddForce` function.

11. Modify the `AddForce` call in your `FireCannon` function to multiply each of the delta values by 5 as shown:

```
void FireCannon(float xForce, float yForce)
{
    . . .
    newCannonball.rigidbody.AddForce(xForce * 5, yForce * 5,
       0f, ForceMode.Impulse);
}
```

Due to the precision of the OUYA's touchpad when using this method of touch capturing, sometimes two individual swipes are detected when only one was performed. To remedy this, we'll add a simple counter that prevents two cannonballs from being fired in a quick succession.

12. Declare the counter next to your other variables as follows:

```
private int fireCooldown = 0;
```

We'll let the cannon fire a cannonball as long as the cooldown is at zero, but we'll increase the value of fireCooldown as soon as we fire.

13. Add the following lines at the beginning and end of your FireCannon function to implement the previous logic:

```
void FireCannon(float xForce, float yForce)
{
if(fireCooldown > 0)
return;
. . .
newCannonball.rigidbody.AddForce(xForce * 5, yForce * 5,
   0f, ForceMode.Impulse);
fireCooldown = 120;
}
```

We'll subtract 1 from fireCooldown for each frame until it gets back to 0. By setting it to `120` when the cannon fires, it will wait for 120 frames (about two seconds) before firing again.

14. Lastly, add the following lines to your `Update` function to decrease the cooldown value by 1 for each frame if it's above 0 and not ready to be fired yet:

```
void Update()
{
CaptureTouch();

if(fireCooldown > 0)
fireCooldown--;
```

You can now test the game and see the cannonballs being fired in whatever direction the cursor is moving, even straight up:

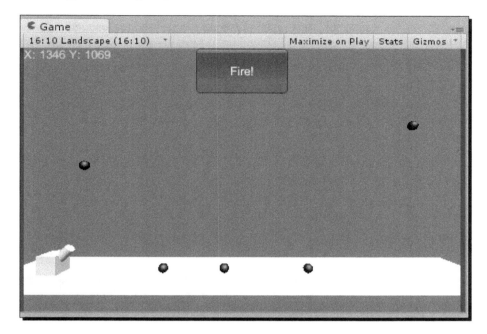

Additionally, the faster you swipe, the farther the cannonball travels.

What just happened?

You've successfully overridden the OUYA cursor's default mouse functionality to create true touch gesture mechanics in your game. By measuring the change in the cursor position and keeping track of separate motions, you can enable your player to "touch" your game and engage them even more.

We're not completely done with our current implementation; we still need to hide the cursor that the OUYA displays by default whenever it receives a touch input.

As we base our touch data on the change in cursor position, the function will cease to work when the cursor hits a border of the screen and cannot further change its position. A future update to the OUYA SDK or Unity may enable you to reset the cursor position on the OUYA, but currently the cursor can only be manipulated on PC builds. When integrating touch into your game, try to do so in a way that won't leave your player stuck if the cursor hits a border.

Have a go hero – capturing touch input over multiple frames

In the previous section, you saw how cursor movement over one frame can affect the direction of force on a cannonball. However, as we only measured the change over one frame, the function is not very precise, and you need to move the cursor very quickly if you want a strong shot.

Use what you've learned about game scripting so far to measure cursor coordinates over multiple frames during a single touch sequence and create a function that averages out each frame's delta change to produce a more precise touch gesture. Here are a couple of tips to get you started:

- It's a smart idea to store the coordinate data collected from each frame in an array so they're all kept together.
- Hint: declare two arrays to store your X and Y coordinates over five frames, as shown in the following code:

```
float[] deltaValuesX = new float [5];
float[] deltaValuesY = new float [5];
```

You can access individual values of the array by putting a bracketed index directly after the name. This is shown in the following example, which prints out the third value in the array:

```
print(deltaValuesX[3]);
```

Hint: to access each element of the array in succession, use a for loop that runs five times with a counter incrementing at each step, and use the counter variable to access the corresponding element. The basic structure is demonstrated in the following code in a for loop that prints the value of each element of the array:

```
for(int i = 0; i < 5; i++)
{
  print(deltaValue[i]);
}
```

- Modify your CaptureTouch function so that it measures delta values even if a swipe is in progress, but make sure to stop it from measuring delta values as soon as the swipe is ended.

Incorporating touch data into your mechanics

Now that you're capturing touch data from the cursor, all that's left is to make the concept complete by turning it from a feature into a full mechanic tied to the game. In this section, we'll hide the default OUYA cursor from displaying while our user swipes to fire a cannonball to try and hit a target on the other end of the level.

Time for action – hiding the cursor on the screen

OUYA's cursor is slightly different than other components of our game in that it's displayed and managed by an unseen Java script that we didn't need to create. This code is a core part of the OUYA SDK, so we can't change it directly; instead, we need to use methods that have been included in the SDK that serve the purpose of safely modifying core functionality.

By default, the cursor appears whenever the cursor is moved, as shown in the following screenshot:

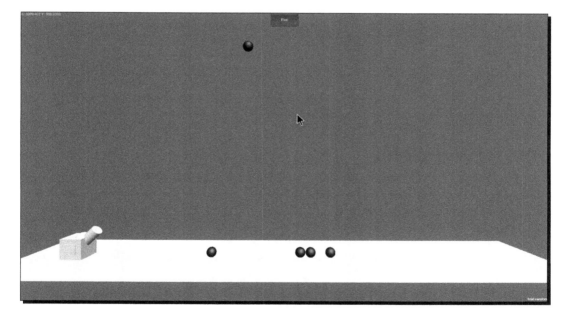

Perform the following steps to hide the cursor on the screen:

1. Create a new function called `HideCursor` in `CursorScript.cs`:

    ```
    void HideCursor()
    {

    }
    ```

2. Add the following line to the `HideCursor` function to call the Java function that hides the cursor graphic:

    ```
    void HideCursor()
    {
        OuyaSDK.OuyaJava.JavaShowCursor(false);
    }
    ```

3. Add a call to `HideCursor` in your `Update` function so that it's called for every frame:

    ```
    void Update()
    {
        HideCursor();
    }
    ```

4. Deploy your game to the OUYA console and swipe the touchpad to fire the cannon.

You'll notice that the cursor no longer appears on the screen when you move it with the touchpad.

What just happened?

The `JavaShowCursor` function that you called from the `OuyaSDK` class is only one of the many ways you can interact with the under-the-hood features of the development kit. The Unity engine can't access or control the OUYA cursor because it's handled by Java, but we can access the cursor indirectly with the ODK.

Now that our touch mechanic is fully implemented, all we need to do is create a target for the player to hit.

Time for action – creating a target for the cannon

To complete our prototype, we'll add a target for the player to attempt to hit with a cannonball and make it change color when they've successfully hit it. Perform the following steps to do so:

1. Create a new **Cube** from the **Hierarchy** window's **Create** menu.

2. Position the cube at 20, 5, 0 so that it's on the opposite end of the plane from the cannon and slightly higher than it.

   Your cube should look as shown in the following screenshot:

   We want our target cube to be a bit larger and easier to see, so we'll make a few more changes to it.

3. Increase the scale of the cube to 3, 3, 3.

4. Create a new **Material**, assign it a unique color, and apply it to your target by clicking-and-dragging it from the **Project** window to the cube in the **Hierarchy** window.

After making the previous changes, your target cube should look as shown in the following screenshot:

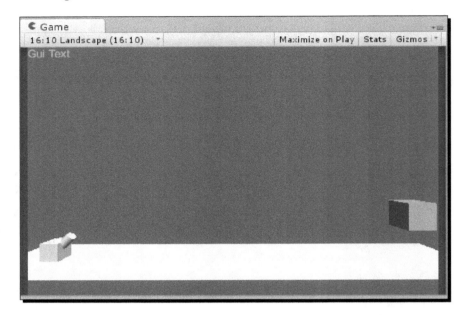

Now that our cube is a clear target, we can script it to react when a cannonball hits it. In full games, hitting a target would do something like increment a point value or load the next level, but for the purposes of our prototype, we'll just make the cube change its color to signify a successful collision.

5. Create a new script called `TargetScript.cs` and open it in your code editor.

6. Add a definition for Unity's built-in collision-checking function `OnCollisionEnter` as shown:

```
void OnCollisionEnter(Collision collidingObj)
{

}
```

7. Add the following line to the `OnCollisionEnter` function to make it turn red when a cannonball collides with it:

```
void OnCollisionEnter(Collision collidingObj)
{
   gameObject.renderer.material.color = Color.red;
}
```

8. Attach `TargetScript.cs` to the target cube by dragging it from your `Code` folder in the **Project** window to the target cube in the **Hierarchy** window or the **Scene** view.

9. Run your game and fire a cannon at the target until you hit it to observe the new collision functionality.

   Once a cannonball hits the target, it will immediately change color to denote a collision, as shown in the following screenshot:

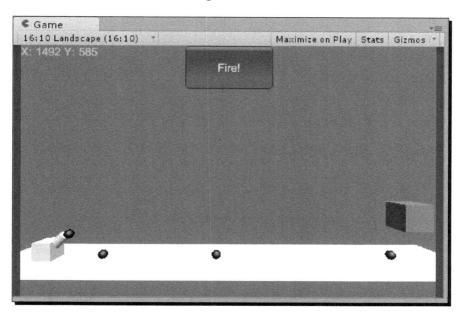

What just happened?

Congratulations, your touch prototype is complete! You've successfully used the basic and advanced touch inputs to make your game more than just a simple button-and-joystick game. Try exploring the touch functionality to make it more robust and precise; the menu and button controls with the touchpad will do your game well, but defining a library of touch gestures in your code base goes above and beyond what is provided to you to work with in the OUYA SDK and will impress your players no end.

Feel free to keep exploring with the cannon prototype and see how far you can push the touch capabilities, but don't edit the core features of the project too much; we'll be returning to this prototype in *Chapter 7, Expanding Your Gameplay with In-App Purchases*, where we'll create different classes of cannonballs that all behave uniquely.

Pop quiz – touching the sky

Q1. How does the touchpad behave by default?

1. A graphical cursor with a menu-clicking ability

2. It doesn't, additional code is required to implement it

3. An invisible touch input reader

Q2. Which of the following restricts advanced touch coding with delta values for OUYA in Unity?

1. Java/C# compatibility

2. Screen borders

3. Always-present graphical cursor

Q3. How can you manipulate parts of the OUYA platform that Unity can't access?

1. Edit the SDK directly

2. You cannot

3. Use external code wrappers provided in the SDK

Summary

Now that you've acquired a taste for the capabilities of touch in OUYA games, you can start creating games that diverge from common controller-based games that don't feature touch such as Xbox 360 and PlayStation 3 games. You've also learned more about manipulating data in both the Unity engine and the OUYA SDK, which can help you create solutions for complex custom systems that don't have pre-written implementations.

In the next chapter, we'll move back to our marble prototype and program a system that will allow us to save data from the game, even after it stops running.

6
Saving Data to Create Longer Games

By now, you've learned all of the basic steps to create fun mechanics in OUYA games, and you can start being creative by playing around with your current knowledge and see if it leads to new discoveries. However, without persistent save data, your creative scope is limited to a single play session, which probably won't be longer than a few hours.

Implementing long-term skill progression and narrative development can do a lot for your game experience, and it keeps players coming back to the game to reach new milestones. Even single-session games such as Canabalt expand their replayability drastically by simply adding in save data for the all-time high score.

We'll accomplish the following goals in this chapter:

◆ Learn how to save game data with the Unity engine

◆ Enhance your prototype from *Chapter 4, Moving Your Player with Controller Input*, by adding collectibles

◆ Save collectible data so that player progress is tracked between play sessions

◆ An introduction to saving persistent data with the OUYA API

Creating collectibles to save

The Unity engine features an incredibly simple saving and loading system that can load your data between sessions in just a few lines of code. The downside of using Unity's built-in data management is that save data will be erased if the game is ever uninstalled from the OUYA console. Later, we'll talk about how to make your data persistent between installations, but for now, we'll set up some basic data-driven values in your marble prototype. However, before we load the saved data, we have to create something to save.

Time for action – creating a basic collectible

Some games use save data to track the total number of times the player has obtained a collectible item. Players may not feel like it's worth gathering collectibles if they disappear when the game session is closed, but making the game track their long-term progress can give players the motivation to explore a game world and discover everything it has to offer. We're going to add collectibles to the marble game prototype you created and save them so that the player can see how many collectibles they've totally gathered over every play session. Perform the following steps to create a collectible:

1. Open your `RollingMarble` Unity project and double-click on the scene that has your level in it.

2. Create a new cylinder from the **Create** menu in your **Hierarchy** menu. Move the cylinder so that it rests on the level's platform. It should appear as shown in the following screenshot:

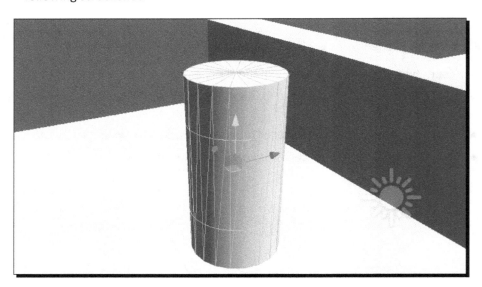

3. We don't want our collectible to look like a plain old cylinder, so manipulate it with the rotate and scale tools until it looks a little more like a coin. Obviously, you'll have a coin model in the final game that you can load, but we can customize and differentiate primitive objects for the purpose of our prototype.

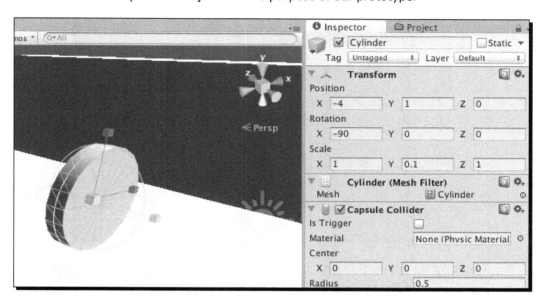

4. Our primitive is starting to look like a coin, but it's still a bland gray color. To make it look a little bit nicer, we'll use Unity to apply a material.

A material tells the engine how an object should appear when it is rendered, including which textures and colors to use for each object. Right now, we'll only apply a basic color, but later on we'll see how it can store different kinds of textures and other data.

Materials can be created and customized in a matter of minutes in Unity, and they're a great way to color simple objects or distinguish primitive shapes from one another.

5. Create a new folder named `Materials` in your **Project** window and right-click on it to create a new material named `CoinMaterial` as shown in the following screenshot:

6. Click on the material that you just created and its properties will appear in the **Inspector** window. Click on the color box next to the **Main Color** property and change it to a yellow color. The colored sphere in the **Material** window will change to reflect how the material will look in real time, as shown in the following screenshot:

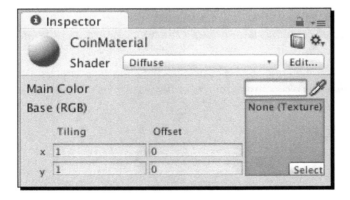

Our collectible coin now has a color, but as we can see from the preview of the sphere, it's still kind of dull. We want our coin to be shiny so that it catches the player's eye, so we'll change the **Shader** type, which dictates how light hits the object.

7. The current **Shader** type on our coin material is **Diffuse**, which basically means it is a softer, nonreflective material. To make the coin shiny, change the **Shader** type to **Specular**. You'll see a reflective flare appear on the sphere preview; adjust the **Shininess** slider to see how different levels of specularity affect the material.

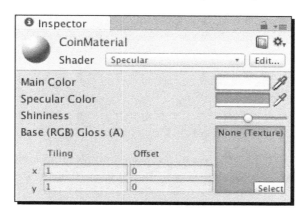

You may have noticed that another color value was added when you changed the material's shader from **Diffuse** to **Specular**; this value affects only the shiny parts of the object. You can make the material shine brighter by changing it from gray to white, or give its shininess a tint by using a completely new color.

8. Attach your material to the collectible object by clicking-and-dragging the material from the **Project** window and releasing it over the object in your scene view. The object will look like the one shown in the following screenshot:

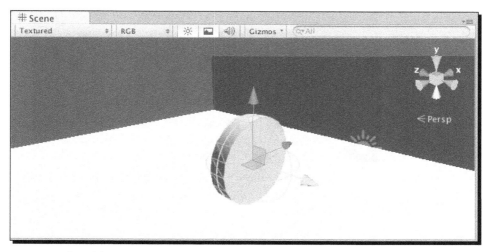

Our collectible coin object now has a unique shape and appearance, so it's a good idea to save it as a prefab.

9. Create a `Prefabs` folder in your **Project** window if you haven't already, and use the folder's right-click menu to create a new blank prefab named `Coin`. Click-and-drag the coin object from the hierarchy to the prefab to complete the link.

We'll add code to the coin later, but we can change the prefab after we initially create it, so don't worry about saving an incomplete collectible. Verify whether the prefab link worked by clicking-and-dragging multiple instances of the prefab from the **Project** window onto the **Scene** view.

What just happened?

Until you start adding 3D models to your game, primitives are a great way to create placeholder objects, and materials are useful for making them look more complex and unique.

Materials add color to objects, but they also contain a shader that affects the way light hits the object. The two most basic shaders are **Diffuse** (dull) and **Specular** (shiny), but there are several other shaders in Unity that can help make your object appear exactly like you want it. You can even code your own shaders using the ShaderLab language, which you can learn on your own using the documentation at http://docs.unity3d.com/Documentation/Components/SL-Reference.html.

Next, we'll add some functionality to your coin to save the collection data.

Have a go hero – make your prototype stand out with materials

As materials are easy to set up with Unity's color picker and built-in shaders, you have a lot of options at your fingertips to quickly make your prototype stand out and look better than a basic grayscale mock-up. Take any of your existing projects and see how far you can push the aesthetic with different combinations of colors and materials.

Keep the following points in mind:

◆ Some shaders, such as **Specular**, have multiple colors that you can assign. Play around with different combinations to create a unique appearance.

◆ There are more shaders available to you than just the ones loaded into a new project; move your mouse over the **Import Package** option in Unity's **Assets** menu and import the **Toon Shading** package to add even more options to your shader collection.

◆ Complex object prefabs made of more than one primitive can have a different material on each primitive. Add multiple materials to a single object to help your user differentiate between its various parts and give your scene more detail.

Try changing the materials used in your scene until you come up with something unique and clean, as shown in the following screenshot of our cannon prototype with custom materials:

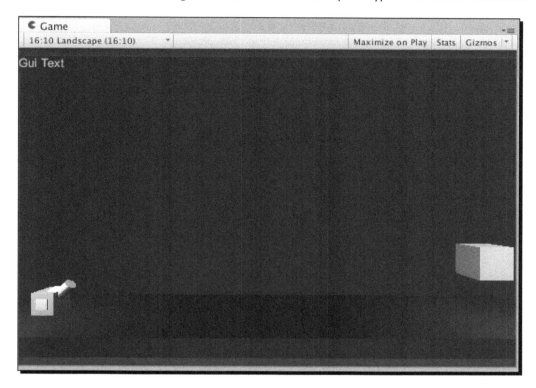

Time for action – scripting the collectible

The first thing we'll script is some basic movement. Typically, the collectibles in games have some basic animation to differentiate them from the static objects in the scene, and it helps the player identify where they are. For our coin, just a constant rotation should suffice to make it stick out. Perform the following steps to script the collectible:

1. Right-click on your `Scripts` folder in the **Project** window and create a new C# script named `CoinRotation.cs`.

2. Double-click on the script to open it in your code editor. Add the following lines to the script's `Update` function:

```
void Update()
{
    gameObject.transform.Rotate(0, 0, 5);
}
```

These lines access whatever the `GameObject` script is attached to and call the `transform` property's `Rotate` function, which takes three parameters (one for each axis of rotation). We want to rotate our coin along the *z* axis, so we added a value of 5 in the **Z** axis parameter field and left the other values as 0.

The `transform` property in every `GameObject` also includes the `Translate` function, which takes the *x*, *y*, and *z* arguments and moves an object along those axes rather than rotating around them.

We don't need anything else from the rotation script; we'll be coding the collectible data on the coin as well, but it's a good idea to keep your scripts separated by purpose, so we'll leave this script as it is and create another one for a more advanced functionality.

3. Save the `CoinRotation.cs` file and attach it to your `Coin` prefab by dragging it from the `Scripts` folder to the prefab. Press play to ensure that your coin now constantly rotates in the game.

Next, we'll add another script that checks whether our marble touches the coin. When we created the primitive cylinder that our coin is based on, a **Collider** component was automatically added to it. Game objects use colliders to detect interaction with other objects in physical space, and they have several customizable properties in our coin's **Inspector** window under the **Capsule Collider** region, as shown in the following screenshot:

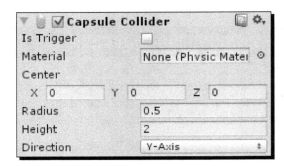

The checkbox next to the **Is Trigger** prompt allows the object to collect the collision data without applying any automatic physical force, which is useful for item pickups and other nonphysical interactions. As we don't want our coin to impact our marble in any way when we collect it, we'll want to set the coin's collider to act as a trigger.

4. Select your `Coin` prefab from the **Project** window, and locate the component labeled **Capsule Collider** in the **Inspector** window. Click on the box to the right of the **Is Trigger** prompt once to activate it.

If you want to make changes to an object prefab, make sure that you apply the change to the prefab (in the **Project** window) rather than an instance of it in the scene (in the **Hierarchy** window). Changes made to individual instances of objects only change that instance, which is useful to differentiate instances, but this can lead to some puzzling inconsistencies if you don't keep the base prefab updated. To update a prefab, click on the **Apply** button in the **Inspector** window, or click-and-drag the updated object from the **Hierarchy** window over to the existing prefab to overwrite it.

The other properties of the collider aren't important to us right now, but they're still relatively straightforward. The **Physics Material** property can accept any of Unity's built-in physical materials such as ice, which changes the way collisions and movement behave. The other position and orientation values all represent what part of the object the attached collider encompasses. When primitive objects create their own colliders, they're initially sized to fit perfectly around the shape, but they can always be adjusted to create a custom collidable area.

5. Test your game in the Unity editor and try to roll your marble into the coin. You'll notice that even though there's an active collider on the coin, it doesn't physically impact the marble at all. This is because we have it set to be a trigger instead of a collision.

   Of course, simply not making an impact isn't enough of a functionality for the coin; we still need to make it interactive.

6. Create a new script labeled `CollectibleScript.cs` in your `Code` folder, and open it in your code editor.

   To handle collision, we'll use one of Unity's built-in functions named `OnTriggerEnter`. This function is available on all objects with colliders, but it doesn't automatically add itself to scripts as the `Start` and `Update` functions do, so the first thing you'll need to do is add it to your new script.

7. Add the following `OnTriggerEnter` function extension to your new script under the `Update` function:

```
void Update()
{

}

void OnTriggerEnter(Collider collidingObj)
{

}
```

The single parameter that the `OnTriggerEnter` function takes is of the type `Collider`, which is a Unity-specific datatype that we can use to access all sorts of information about any collision that occurs, including the position, type, and game objects involved.

We'll test this function using a simple print statement to output some text to the Unity editor. Add the following call to Unity's `print` function in your `OnTriggerEnter` function:

```
void OnTriggerEnter(Collider collidingObj)
{
    print(collidingObj.transform.position);
}
```

8. The only thing left to do is complete the link between your coin and your new script. Click-and-drag `CollectibleScript.cs` and release it over your `Coin` prefab to add it to all the instances of that prefab.

9. Click on the play button in the Unity editor, and roll your marble into the coin as shown in the following screenshot:

(-5.0, 0.7, 0.0)

You'll notice that as soon as the collision occurs, a print statement will appear in the bottom-left corner of the Unity editor, which outputs the location of the collision.

Every time you roll away from the coin and then roll back into it, it will reprint the collision data because the `OnTriggerEnter` function is called every time a collision is entered between two objects with colliders.

In addition to the `OnTriggerEnter` function, the Unity API also contains an `OnTriggerExit` function that gets called when two objects separate from a collision, and an `OnTriggerStay` collision that gets called for every frame that a collision occurs. Each of these are useful in their own way when creating your game.

In the case of our coin, we don't want our player to be able to pick it up more than once, so we'll tell the coin to delete itself as soon as a player collects it.

10. Add the following lines to the `OnTriggerEnter` function in your `CollectibleScript.cs` file:

```
void OnTriggerEnter(Collider collidingObj)
{
  print(collidingObj.transform.position);
  Destroy(this.gameObject);
}
```

If you test the scene in the Unity editor again, the coin will disappear as soon as the marble touches it. Next, the coin will need to notify the game somehow that it's been collected, and then we can save that data so that the total number of collectibles is persistent.

What just happened?

Now is a good time to look back at what you've done so far. With the two scripts that you wrote, you've made your coin a fully functioning object in the game world.

Even though the code contained between the two scripts could have been put into one, it's a good practice as a developer to keep your scripts separated by purpose, so if you ever want to change the specific functionality of one aspect of an object, you can change that aspect's code without having to look through or change anything else.

You also utilized Unity's built-in `OnTriggerEnter` function for the first time. This function is extremely useful for handling interactions between objects in the game world, and the collider parameter provides a wealth of information about both objects involved in the collision, which you can use to collect data about your game.

There's a function similar to `OnTriggerEnter` that works with non-trigger colliding objects; this is useful for colliding objects that make an impact, such as bullets or balls. This function is named `OnCollisionEnter`, and the only thing that differentiates it from `OnTriggerEnter` is that it takes a `Collision` type as the parameter and not a `Collider` type. The collision data carries a few more values with it, such as impact force and momentum.

The only thing left to complete the collection event is tell the player that they've collected something, and we'll do this by accessing the player's script from the collider data.

Time for action – accessing the scripts on other objects

The only existing script on our marble right now is the input script, so create another one that will be responsible for handling the collection data. Perform the following steps to access the scripts:

1. Create a new file named `PlayerCollection.cs` in your `Scripts` folder and open it in your code editor.

2. Add the following variable and function to your code, above and below the `Start` and `Update` functions, respectively:

```
private int totalCoins = 0;

// Use this for initialization
void Start()
{

}

// Update is called once per frame
void Update()
{

}

public void CollectCoin()
{
  totalCoins++;
  print(totalCoins);
}
```

Let's look at the two things you just added to your script. We set the `int` variable to `private` because this script is the only one that needs to edit that value, but we added a `public` function that increments the value by one.

This method is better than directly accessing a public variable on another script because making variables private ensures that objects interact with the data only in ways you've defined.

Next, we'll call the `CollectCoin` function from the coin as soon as it's collected. We'll do this by accessing the player object with the `collider` variable in the `OnTriggerEnter` function.

3. Open your `CollectibleScript.cs` file, and add the following line to the `OnTriggerEnter` function:

```
void OnTriggerEnter(Collider collidingObj)
{
  print(collidingObj.transform.position);
  collidingObj.GetComponent<PlayerCollection>().CollectCoin();
  Destroy(this.gameObject);
}
```

4. Test your new code in the editor and ensure that the print statement you wrote to display the total number of coins appears when the coin is destroyed.

5. Try adding several coins to the map and rolling into all of them to see the print statement's value get higher with each coin you collect.

Now the marble and coins should appear as shown in the following screenshot:

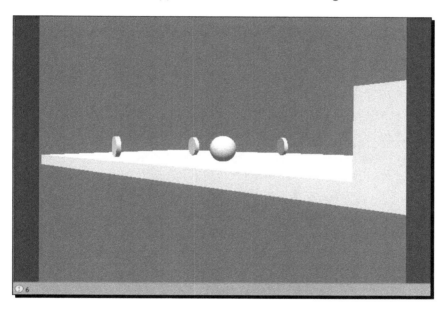

What just happened?

A lot of games require an immense amount of interaction between objects, so cohesion between code systems is a must. Unity's `GetComponent` function is a great way to access values from other scripts on any object in your scene.

Using the data returned from a trigger collision using Unity's built-in collision detection, we got the `PlayerCollection` data from the colliding marble game object and were able to call a public function that incremented a private variable representative of the total number of coins collected by it.

Later, you'll learn other ways to access other game objects from within a script; but for now, we'll focus on saving the data that you've already collected so that it reloads whenever the game is started.

At this point, the number resets whenever you stop the game and press play again, so next we'll save the data every time a new coin is collected.

Saving data with the Unity engine

Now that our prototype features a collectible that we can save, we need to actually program the saving operation using Unity's built-in data storage methods. In this section, you'll save data and see it loaded even after you close the game and reopen it.

Time for action – saving data with PlayerPrefs

We're finally ready to save and load data to the player's collection class. For this, we'll be using Unity's `PlayerPrefs` class in code.

1. Open the `PlayerCollection.cs` file in your code editor and add the following lines to your `CollectCoin` function:

```
public void CollectCoin()
{
  totalCoins++;
  print(totalCoins);
  PlayerPrefs.SetInt("TotalCoins", totalCoins);
}
```

It's as simple as that! Let's examine what this new line actually does. We're calling the `SetInt` function from the `PlayerPrefs` class because the data we're saving is an integer value. However, `PlayerPrefs` also contains functions to save floating-point values and strings.

No matter what kind of data you're saving, the parameters for the saving function are generally the same. The first value is a text string that represents a **key** or a way to label the data you're saving so that you can access it later.

The second parameter is the data you're saving with that key, be it an integer, string, or float. Of course, sometimes you may want to save data that doesn't fit any of those three datatypes; for example, the C# `Color` datatype. In such instances, you would need to program a way to translate the value into one of the accepted datatypes. One way to do this would be to program a function that saves and loads integers for the color value (red = 1, orange = 2, and so on).

Next, we'll set up our `PlayerCollection` class so that it loads in our saved value as soon as the game starts.

2. Add a line to the `Start` function in `CollectibleScript.cs` as follows:

```
// Use this for initialization
void Start()
{
  totalCoins = PlayerPrefs.GetInt("TotalCoins");
}
```

As the `Start` function of `PlayerCollection` gets called once at the beginning of our game, we can use it to assign our last saved value to the `totalCoins` variable to ensure that we pick up right where we left off.

3. Add a `print` statement to the `Start` function, which will print out the value of the `totalCoins` variable right after it's loaded:

```
// Use this for initialization
void Start()
{
  totalCoins = PlayerPrefs.GetInt("TotalCoins");
  print("Total coins on load: " + totalCoins);
}
```

4. Click on play, collect some coins, stop the game, and then click on play again. You'll see your number of previously collected coins in Unity's editor output, confirming that your save and load operations are now fully functional.

What just happened?

At this point, the data that you save is completely up to you. You can use integers, strings, and float datatypes in tandem with the saving and loading functions to record virtually any value that needs to be carried through to every play session.

Just being able to use Unity's saving and loading expands the scope of any of your games greatly because you can now set goals that take longer than a standard play session to complete and not worry about your player losing their progress.

The only thing your prototype is lacking now is a visual representation of the data that you've saved. To show the total number of coins collected without using Unity's output window, we'll use something called `GUIText`.

Time for action – setting up a GUI Text object

The Unity engine features a component/object type named GUIText, which can display raw text and numerical values as stylized text on your game's viewport. We can write a script for a new GUIText component that will determine the total number of coins collected and update the displayed text with that count. Perform the following steps to set up GUIText:

1. Make a new GUIText object from the **Create** menu of your **Hierarchy** window.

You'll notice that the GUIText position is set to 0.5, 0.5, 0 by default. However, it displays in the middle of the game window regardless of your position. That's because a GUIText position value doesn't affect its global position, only its location on the screen.

We want GUIText to appear in the upper-right corner so that it doesn't obscure the center of our view, so we'll change the coordinates to the maximum **X** and **Y** values. The **Z** value of GUIText represents the depth, which won't become apparent until you have multiple texts, when the texts with the greatest depth will be displayed behind all the others.

2. Set the position of the GUIText component to 1, 1, 0.

Unfortunately, even though the text's new position is perfectly situated in the upper-right corner, it's not visible on the screen because the anchor of the text is at the upper-left corner. We can fix this by adjusting the anchor of the text to be at the far right instead of the far left.

3. Edit the **Anchor** property of GUIText in the **Inspector** window to be **upper right**.

4. The text looks a little small as well, so increase the font size to 20.

Your GUIText component should now look something similar to the following **Inspector** window:

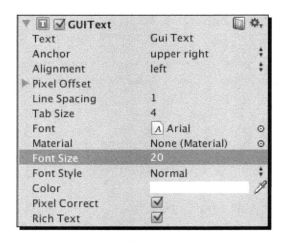

Now all that the `GUIText` component needs is the text to display, and we'll read that data from the `PlayerCollection` class. However, because a collision never occurs between `GUIText` and the marble that holds `PlayerCollection`, we need a different way to access that data.

Fortunately, this process is easily accomplished with Unity's tag system, which is a way that a developer can explicitly define and locate identifiers.

5. Select your `Marble` prefab in the **Project** window, and select **Add Tag...** in the **Tag** menu as shown in the following screenshot:

6. Select the empty text box next to **Element 0**, and type in `Marble` to add it as a new tag, as shown in the following screenshot:

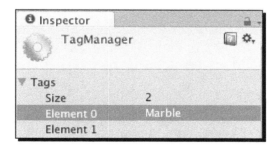

Even though you've now created the tag, it doesn't automatically apply to your marble, so we'll need to go back to the marble's prefab and tag it.

7. Select your `Marble` prefab, and change the tag to `Marble`, as shown in the following screenshot:

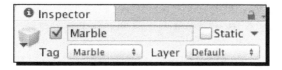

Now that your marble is properly tagged, we can access it in code. However, right now we only have a function in `PlayerCollection.cs` that sets the total number of coins, and we don't have a function that collects it.

8. Add the following function to your `PlayerCollection` class:

```
public int GetTotalCoins()
{
  return totalCoins;
}
```

9. Create a new script named `CollectibleGUI.cs`, attach it to the `GUIText` object in your scene, and then open it in the code editor.

10. Add the following lines to the `Update` function so that our text object updates every frame:

```
void Update()
{
  guiText.text =
    GameObject.FindGameObjectWithTag("Marble").GetComponent
      <PlayerCollection>().GetTotalCoins().ToString();
}
```

Don't be intimidated by the length of the line of code you just wrote; it's wordy, but the operation is relatively simple. Every frame, we find the value of the `GetTotalCoins` function based on the game object that we gave the `Marble` tag to. We then assign that to the `guiText.text` property for every frame so that our total number stays updated as we play.

11. Test your game to see how the `GUIText` component responds to the collection of coins.

What just happened?

You now have the means to convey numerical data to the player using text onscreen, which is very important for acclimating the player and giving them the information they need (or want) to play your game.

You also learned an alternate method to access scripts on objects in the game world using Unity's tag system. You can have as many custom tags in your game as you want—there are also a decent number of predefined tags to set—and those are useful to organize objects for easy access later.

Now that your saved data is displayed to the user, your save system is fully implemented. Feel free to get creative and try different approaches to perform the same basic functions; code can always be refactored and optimized, and the saving/loading methods in this book are just a couple of the myriad of ways you can structure a persistent data system.

Using save data in multiple scenes

So far, the save data you've interacted with has been stored and loaded by the same scene: the main game scene. However, as save data can be loaded anywhere within a project, we can easily create a system that saves in one scene and loads in another. We'll attempt this by returning to the cannon game prototype and adding a high score scene that displays whenever the game is won. The score will be a numerical value representing how many cannonballs it took the player to hit the target, with lower numbers being displayed higher up in the rankings.

Time for action – counting cannonballs

As with all data operations, the first step is to create a variable that stores the data you want to interact with. To count the number of cannonballs that the player fires, we'll need to use an integer variable with a script that increments the count by one every time the FireCannon function is called. Perform the following steps to count cannonballs:

1. Create a new C# script named ScoreKeeper, and attach it to your Cannon prefab.

2. Automatically add the script to all future instances of your Cannon prefab by clicking on **Apply** in the **Inspector** window after you attach the script.

3. Open the ScoreKeeper script, declare an int variable named numCannonballsFired, and initialize it to 0 in the Start function as shown in the following code:

```
private int numCannonballsFired;
void Start()
{
  numcannonballsFired = 0;
}
```

Next, we need a public function that will increment the integer value by one every time it's called.

4. Create a new function named IncrementCount and add a line that increases the count of numCannonballsFired so that your function looks like the following code:

```
void IncrementCount()
{
  numCannonballsFired++;
}
```

Now that our function is set up, we need to create a way to call it when a cannonball is fired. We could set up an external object reference like we did with Unity's tag system earlier in this chapter, but there's another way we could call this function that would fit our needs just fine: we could turn it into a static function.

Static functions are functions that can be called whether or not any instances of an object with the function attached are present, and they're completely independent of the values of individual instantiations of that object or script. The only values that static functions can interact with are static variables; otherwise, discrepancies could occur with differing values of duplicate variables on separate instantiations.

Functions and variables can easily be made static by preceding them with the `static` keyword.

5. Convert your `numCannonballsFired` variable to static by inserting the `static` keyword after the `private` keyword:

```
private static int numCannonballsFired;
```

6. Convert your `IncrementCount` function to static by inserting the `static` keyword before the `void` keyword:

```
public static void IncrementCount()
{
    numCannonballsFired++;
}
```

Now the function is ready to be called.

7. Attach the `ScoreKeeper` script to the `Cannon` prefab and apply changes.

8. Open the `CannonScript` file to add a call to `IncrementCount` in the `FireCannon` function.

As previously mentioned, when calling a static function, a reference to an instance of that object type isn't necessary. Instead, the function can be called using the complete class name.

9. Add a call to `IncrementCount` at the very end of the `FireCannon` function, as shown in the following code:

```
void FireCannon(float xForce, float yForce)
{
    ...
    ScoreKeeper.IncrementCount();
}
```

What just happened?

Your `ScoreKeeper` script now keeps track of the number of cannonballs your player fires. You could have used standard functions to achieve this by making them public and adding a reference to them from the `CannonScript` file, but instead you made the variable and function static, allowing you to call it from anywhere using just the `ScoreKeeper` class name followed directly by the function name.

Next, we'll create a way to read that value when the game is complete and check if it's a better score than the three best scores.

Time for action – checking high scores in a new scene

The first thing we need is a way to store the high score whenever the level ends. This means we'll need to get the number of cannonballs fired at the end of a round and create a `PlayerPrefs` entry for it. We'll do this by creating a static function to return the total number of cannonballs fired in the script and calling it from the target whenever it's hit. The steps to do so are as follows:

1. Create a new static function called `GetCannonballCount` in the `ScoreKeeper` class, and add a line that returns the integer value of `numCannonballsFired`, as shown in the following code:

```
public static int GetCannonballCount()
{
  return numCannonballsFired;
}
```

2. Open your `TargetScript` file, and add the following lines to its `OnCollisionEnter` function to save the player's score, which we'll access later from the high score script:

```
void OnCollisionEnter(Collision collidingObj)
{
  gameObject.renderer.material.color = Color.red;
  PlayerPrefs.SetInt("NewScore",
    ScoreKeeper.GetCannonballCount());
}
```

Your value is now being saved properly, so we can create a new scene to create and display a high score list and access the value from there.

3. Open Unity's **File** menu and click on **New Scene**.
4. Save your scene as `HighScoreScreen` in your `Scenes` folder.
5. Create a new `GUI Text` object in your scene, and position it in the middle of the screen by setting its **Anchor** setting to **middle center** and its **Alignment** setting to **center** in the **Inspector** window.

6. Set the font color to yellow in the **Inspector** window.

When you're finished, your **Inspector** window should look like the following screenshot:

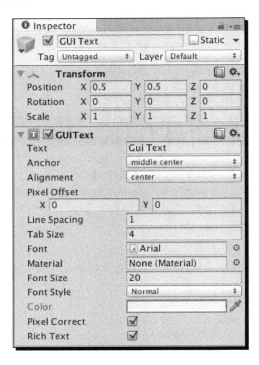

7. Create a new C# script called `HighScoreText` in your `Scripts` folder and open it in your code editor.

8. Create a new function called `ReadHighScores`, defined as follows:

```
void ReadHighScores
{

}
```

The first thing our function needs to do before collecting and displaying the high scores is check whether the latest score has beaten any of the old values. We'll do this by checking three score values in `PlayerPrefs` in order of best to worst and replace the value if the latest score is less than the saved score or there is no saved score yet (which would return a value of 0).

9. Add the following lines to your `ReadHighScores` function to check the three high score slots, and insert the new score if necessary:

```
void ReadHighScores
{
  int latestScore = PlayerPrefs.GetInt("NewScore");

  if(latestScore < PlayerPrefs.GetInt("ScoreOne") ||
    PlayerPrefs.GetInt("ScoreOne") == 0)
  {
    PlayerPrefs.SetInt("ScoreOne",latestScore);
  }
  else if(latestScore < PlayerPrefs.GetInt("ScoreTwo") ||
    PlayerPrefs.GetInt("ScoreTwo") == 0)
  {
    PlayerPrefs.SetInt("ScoreTwo",latestScore);
  }
  else if(latestScore < PlayerPrefs.GetInt("ScoreThree") ||
    PlayerPrefs.GetInt("ScoreThree") == 0)
  {
    PlayerPrefs.SetInt("ScoreThree",latestScore);
  }
}
```

10. Add a call to `ReadHighScores` to the `Start` function of the `HighScoreText` script to check the data as soon as the high score list is loaded:

```
void Start()
{
  ReadHighScores();
}
```

What just happened?

You just wrote a function that checks the player's latest score whenever the game ends and stores it as a high score if it's better than any of the existing high score values. You saved this data in your main game scene, but you're able to read it from the `HighScoreScreen` scene because the data saved with `PlayerPrefs` can be accessed from any scene across multiple play sessions.

All that's left is to display the three high score values after checking them using the `GUI Text` object that we created.

Time for action – displaying high score values

We haven't done anything complicated with GUI Text objects, but they can be powerful and versatile with the proper formatting, so now we'll go over a few tricks you can use to cleanly display three different scores in a list format using only one GUI Text object. Perform the following steps to display high score values:

1. Attach your HighScoreText script to your GUI Text object by clicking-and-dragging it over the GUI Text object in the **Hierarchy** window.

2. Create a new function called DisplayHighScores in the HighScoreText script as shown:

```
void DisplayHighScores()
{

}
```

By default, a GUI Text object displays information in a straight line of text, but what we want is something similar to a list. To achieve this, we'll use what's called an escape character or a special character in the middle of a string that dictates how it's processed or displayed. In this case, we'll be using \n, which creates a new line whenever it's called. While escape characters can be inserted directly into strings, they won't be displayed with the rest of the regular characters; they are only directions for the engine and won't be visible to your player.

3. Add the following lines to your DisplayHighScores function to show all three high score values formatted into a list:

```
void DisplayHighScores()
{
guiText.text = "First: " +
  PlayerPrefs.GetInt("ScoreOne").ToString() + "\nSecond: " +
    PlayerPrefs.GetInt("ScoreTwo").ToString() + "\nThird: " +
      PlayerPrefs.GetInt("ScoreThree").ToString();
}
```

Although the function text in the previous code may seem jumbled and incoherent, it's actually pretty simple; we're just making one long string that converts each score into string characters, labels them in order, and uses the \n escape character to create a new line for each entry.

4. Add a call to `DisplayHighScores` to the `Start` function of your `HighScoreText` script that displays the high score values using the `GUI Text` object directly after reading them:

```
void Start()
{
ReadHighScores();
DisplayHighScores();
}
```

5. Press the **Play** button to test your high score functionality and ensure that your text is being displayed properly.

Your formatted text should look similar to the following screenshot:

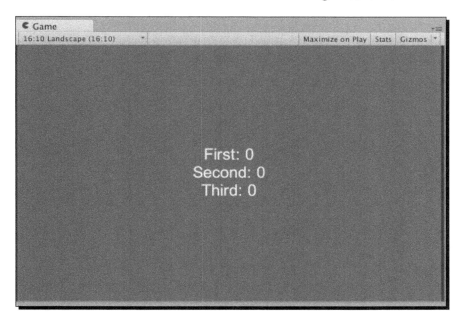

What just happened?

You're now successfully displaying the high score values that your `HighScoreText` script collects in a single `GUI Text` object. You used the `\n` escape character to format the `GUI Text` object to look more like a list, an invaluable trick that can save you a lot of time and help you avoid having to make a different `GUI Text` object for each line you want to display.

The data that your `HighScoreText` script reads is saved from the other scene, demonstrating the full potential of the saving and loading methods of `PlayerPrefs`. Now that you've mastered using `PlayerPrefs` to save whatever data you'd like, we'll take a brief look at the other method available to you to save data: the OUYA API.

Have a go hero – adding a reset button to your high score list

Right now, your high score list will keep the same scores until the end of time (or at least until you uninstall the game from your OUYA). However, you have all of the knowledge you need to create a reset button that clears the values and lets a new set of players shine with fresh high score values. Give it a try!

The following are a few hints to get you started:

- Create the button by encapsulating the `GUI.Button` function within an `if` statement, like you did for the **Fire!** button in the cannon prototype that you created in *Chapter 5, Enhancing Your Game with Touch Dynamics*.

- There's no function to clear a saved value, so instead just use the `PlayerPrefs.SetInt` function to set the function to `0` manually.

- Remember to write all of your GUI functionality within the `OnGUI` function in your `HighScoreText` script.

The following screenshot shows a reset button:

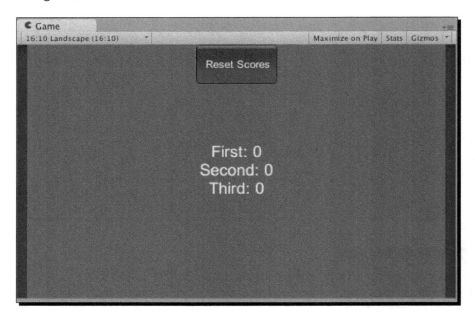

Saving data with the OUYA API

You may remember from the beginning of the chapter that Unity's storage method isn't the only one that you can use to save data. OUYA features its own storage API that can be used to save data with keys just like Unity, but the purpose is slightly different.

Unity's saving mechanism is great because it handles storage and organization of the files all on its own and can be easily accessed using keys. However, if you were to uninstall the game from OUYA or your computer, the saves would no longer be present as they're tied to the project files.

OUYA's storage API, on the other hand, makes sure that the data remains in place even if the game is uninstalled. That way, if a player uninstalls a game that they've made progress on but then reinstall it later, their game will load the OUYA API's saved data from the original installation.

So why not just use OUYA's storage API all the time? For one, it can only store values as strings. You could theoretically save any aspect of a game using strings, but it would require a lot more scripting on your end because strings have to be parsed into integers or floats before they represent any numerical value.

Additionally, if the OUYA API tries to save data from another app and it runs out of room, it may delete some old saves from an uninstalled game to make room. This doesn't happen a lot, but it's too risky to put in-game data in such a volatile place, especially if the difference could mean hours of play time.

Due to its specific purpose and unique constraints, the OUYA storage API is generally used to store data from downloadable content that expands an existing game. Representing this data with a string is fine because you'll most likely want downloadable content to be represented by a plain text word or phrase anyway. Also, it's okay if old data is deleted automatically by the OUYA because downloaded content can always be reacquired using the receipt.

Pop quiz – saving (and loading) the day

Q1. If you wanted to add a new component to a prefab that had already been instantiated at least once in your game, where would you apply the change?

1. In a current instantiation of the prefab
2. In the prefab itself in the **Project** window

Q2. Which of the following saving/loading requirements are best suited for the OUYA storage API?

1. High score/leaderboards
2. Prepurchased DLC
3. User profile

Q3. Which of the following saving/loading requirements are best suited for Unity's `PlayerPrefs` storage method?

1. Unlocked power-ups
2. Purchased content
3. Configuration settings

Q4. If you wanted to collect data from an instantaneous collision between a ball and a hard surface, which function would you use?

1. `OnTriggerEnter`
2. `OnTriggerStay`
3. `OnCollisionEnter`
4. `OnCollisionStay`

Q5. If you wanted to measure how long two triggers overlap with each other, which function would you use?

1. `OnCollisionExit`
2. `OnTriggerStay`
3. `OnCollisionStay`
4. `OnTriggerExit`

Summary

In this chapter, you built a unique collectible game object using primitives and basic materials, saved it to a prefab, and made its instantiations collectible and savable.

You collected coins by calling Unity's `GetComponent` function from the coin's script to access a collection script on the player. `GetComponent` is an extremely useful tool in the Unity engine that allows for substantial communications between two unrelated game objects, so get used to using it.

Finally, you scripted a system that counts the number of coins collected from each play session and adds them to a running total that's loaded every time the game starts. Incorporating save data into your game is essential to expanding your game's scope as it allows you to potentially develop a narrative and skill progression over several sessions rather than giving the player a short, one-shot repetitive experience such as Solitaire.

Next, we'll expand your game further by creating unlockable content that can be purchased by players on the OUYA marketplace. We'll store the data securely and ensure it persists between installations by using OUYA's storage API, which exists primarily to handle downloadable content and permanent settings.

7
Expanding Your Gameplay with In-app Purchases

In the previous chapter, Chapter 6, Saving Data to Create Longer Games, you learned how to expand your game with the saving and loading functionality using Unity's data storage tools. We also briefly touched on saving data with the OUYA API and why it's not ideal to save data related to your gameplay or user experience. OUYA's storage API is perfect, however, for tracking in-app purchases. In this chapter, you'll learn how to make your game more complex and dynamic using in-app purchases while letting your user choose which elements they want to purchase.

The latest generation of games brought with it a new revolution that changed games and re-playability forever: downloadable content, or DLC. As a developer, if you want to explore a new direction or add more features to a game that's already been released, you can upload it as DLC and your players can unlock the content by purchasing it in the marketplace.

DLC also provides a solution for players to pick and choose the features of the game they want to use. For instance, consider the *Texas Hold'em* poker game that featured two downloadable packages: one that enabled additional Five-card stud rules and one that enabled Omaha rules. Instead of being packaged in the main game and sold at a bundle price, the player can pay a small price for the core game and then download Five-card stud and/or Omaha only if they wish. Putting certain features of your game into separate downloadable packages will make more people willing to try your game, and features in packages that would normally overlap can instead be applied à la carte for a custom player experience.

In this chapter, we'll create a few different features to add to the cannonball game prototype we began in *Chapter 5, Enhancing Your Game with Touch Dynamics*. We'll discuss the following points:

◆ The different kinds of in-app purchases

◆ Setting up a product on the OUYA developer portal

◆ Coding in-app purchasing in your game

◆ Adding polish with Unity Asset Store packages

◆ Pricing your in-app purchases

◆ Monetization models

You'll need to use the OUYA developer portal to add products to your game before coding them, so we'll briefly review the developer portal in this chapter as well.

The different kinds of in-app purchases

As noted in *Chapter 1, Experiencing the OUYA*, the OUYA console was built around a free-to-try model that every game uploaded to the marketplace must adhere to. This means that your game must function at some level without the player having to purchase anything, which lets them determine whether they enjoy the game without having to purchase it based solely on the marketplace page. If the player enjoys the demo, they can unlock the game's full functionality by purchasing it from within the game.

The following is a screenshot of the game *MirrorMoon EP*, which features an option to unlock the full game from the pause menu:

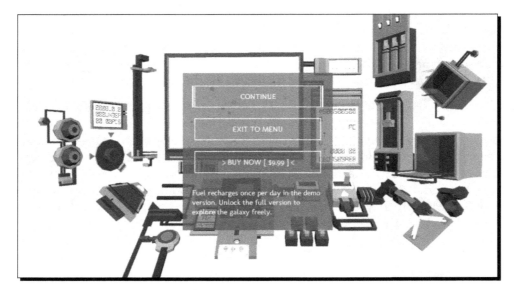

Not all games have in-app purchasing in them, but a majority of those that do feature the "full game unlock" purchase option. One-time purchases such as a full game unlock are called **entitlements**.

Entitlements

Entitlements can only be purchased once per account and always remain tied to the buyer's account even if the game is uninstalled and then reinstalled. True to the name, these purchases entitle the user to the content forever.

Some examples of possible entitlement products include:

◆ Full game unlocks
◆ New level packs
◆ Character skins
◆ Additional items and weapons

Consumables

Consumable items, unlike entitlements, are only usable for a limited amount of time or a certain number of uses. Consumables should never be required to complete your game, but they're good for letting your player take a shortcut or get past a hard section of the game if they want a little help. Imagine, for instance, a level-based game where you need to complete one level before advancing to the next; you could create a consumable item that allows the player to skip one level of their choosing, allowing them to buy it whenever they encounter a level that's too tricky.

Other games offer consumables that provide large amounts of in-game currency as a way to exchange money for what would otherwise require hours of gameplay. One such game on the OUYA marketplace, *Guns'n'Glory WW2*, features a page where you can buy Glory Coins in different bundle amounts as shown in the following screenshot:

The following are some other examples of consumable products:

- ◆ Level skips
- ◆ Single-use power-ups
- ◆ Special ammunition
- ◆ Time-limited upgrades

 Consumable products are one of the most profitable ways to monetize your game because there isn't a limit on how many consumables each user can purchase, but be careful not to make them too powerful or too expensive because players may think the game's main purpose is to make money.

Setting up a product on the OUYA developer portal

In this section, we'll take what you've learned so far about in-app purchasing to create a series of products for your cannonball prototype that you created in *Chapter 5*, *Enhancing Your Game with Touch Dynamics*. These products will include an entitlement that unlocks a full version of the game and several consumables that add different abilities to the cannonballs you fire.

Time for action – preparing your game for in-app purchasing

In-app purchasing (commonly referred to as IAP in developer documentation) requires a properly configured project to work correctly. The first step of ensuring your configuration is making sure the `OuyaGameObject` has your developer ID in it. Perform the following steps to include in-app purchasing in a game:

1. Open a web browser and navigate to `https://devs.ouya.tv/developers`.
2. Use your OUYA account information to log in to the portal.

   After logging in, your developer UUID will appear on the portal splash screen, depicted as a green highlight as shown in the following screenshot:

3. Copy the **UUID** value into your clipboard so that you can paste it later.

4. Open your `TouchCannon` Unity project.

5. Click on `OuyaGameObject` in the **Hierarchy** window to display it in the **Inspector** window.

   `OuyaGameObject` contains a field for you to paste your developer UUID into, as shown in the following screenshot:

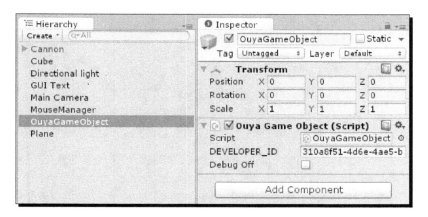

Now that your game is properly linked to your developer ID, you'll need to create an entry for the game on the developer portal.

6. Return to your web browser and click on the **Games** tab on the toolbar at the top of the developer portal.

7. Click on the **Add a Game** link to proceed to the game creation page.

8. Fill out the required information for your cannon game and click on **Save**.

After your game has been created, you'll notice a button next to its entry on the **My Games** page labeled **Signing Key**.

9. Click on the **Download** button underneath the label and save the key in your project directory under `Assets/Plugins/Android/res/raw`.

Your signing key gives your project access to the list of products on the developer portal, so now is a good time to create your first product.

10. Click on the **Products** tab on the toolbar at the top of the developer portal.

11. Click on the dialog that says **New Product** to begin creating and configuring a product for your game.

If you haven't fully completed the developer information page on your own yet, it will ask you to submit payment information and tax documents that ensure validity.

12. Click the on **Payment Info** link to proceed to the page where you can set your bank information. This account is where all of the money made from your in-app purchases will be transferred to.

13. Fill out the requested information. Make sure that the **Location** field is properly set to **US** or **International** (information required differs between the two).

The payment information page for US residents is shown below:

As you can see, not much information is required; the only two numbers required are the routing number and the account number. The account number is specific to your account only and can be found on your bank's website or by contacting your bank. The routing number is shared by all members of a bank in a certain region and can be found by simply searching the web for the routing number for your state or region.

14. Save your information and return to the **Developer Info** page.

15. Click on the **Tax Documents** link to proceed with the required legal paperwork to earn money on the OUYA marketplace.

The tax document you'll be required to fill out depends on your citizenship status, but the **Tax Documents** page will help you find the right one and let you submit it on the same page. Unlike the payment information, your tax information needs to be reviewed by the OUYA team, and they will send you an e-mail as soon as you've been cleared to start accepting purchases.

Once you finally reach the configuration page for a new product, the portal will let you define several different values for that product.

16. Set the **Identifier** value to **E_FullGame**.

The identifier is what we'll use to interact with this item in code. Note that we prefaced the identifier with the letter E, which we'll use to represent entitlement products.

17. Set the **Name** value to **Full Game Unlock**.

The name value is the forward-facing counterpart of our identifier; it's what our player will see when they're browsing the in-app purchases.

18. Set the **Price** value to $0.99 and the **Type** value to Entitlement.

The price here doesn't really matter because we're just creating this product for practice, but when you're adding products to any of your full games, make sure and think hard about this price before you set it.

 Whatever be the price of your purchases, OUYA will take a 30 percent cut of the profits as a marketplace hosting fee. Make sure to take this into account if you're trying to set a monetary goal.

What just happened?

You've created your first product on the OUYA developer portal after taking care of the necessary tax documents and payment information. We haven't actually added the product to the game or written any code yet, but as you've seen, a little work is needed to get your game ready to handle purchases.

Above all, it's important to make sure the developer ID value on `OuyaGameObject` in your scene matches the UUID on the splash page of the developer portal and that the signing key of the game you're working on has been downloaded and stored in `Assets/Plugins/ Android/res/raw`. Without either of these configured correctly, you will not be able to sell your products in your game.

Coding in-app purchasing in your game

In this section, you'll write the code to access the products you create on the OUYA developer portal. All of your products can be read and displayed using the OUYA ODK in Unity, so we'll first create a script that frames a purchase screen and then add elements to it.

Time for action – creating a purchase screen

To sell our product in our game, we first need a screen that offers the option for users to buy it. As a developer, you can put the purchase screen anywhere, but for this demonstration, we'll add it to a pause screen. Perform the following steps to create a purchase screen:

1. Create an empty `GameObject` to hold our pause screen code by clicking on **Create Empty** in the **GameObject** menu on Unity's toolbar.

2. Name the new object `PauseManager` in the **Hierarchy** window.

    Your new object should now appear in the **Inspector** and **Hierarchy** windows as shown in the following screenshot:

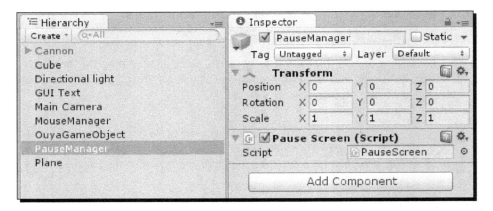

    Next, we'll create the pause screen window that will contain the purchase button.

3. Add a new **GUI Texture** component to your `PauseManager` object by selecting it from the **Rendering** category in the **Add Component** menu.

4. Use your preferred image editor to create a basic texture that reads **PAUSED** at the top and apply it to your **GUI Texture** component.

   Make sure your texture is positioned at the proper scale and offset in the center of the screen and is easily visible as shown in the following screenshot:

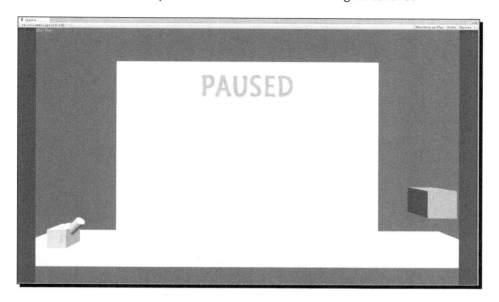

   The pause screen texture shown in the previous screenshot is a 800 x 600 image with -400 and -300 as the offset values for **X** and **Y**, respectively.

5. Create a new script called `PauseScreen.cs`, attach it to your `PauseManager` object, and open it in your code editor.

6. Add the following variable to your `PauseScreen` script above your `Start` function, which we will use to toggle the display of the pause screen on and off:

```
bool isPaused = false;

// Use this for initialization
void Start ()
{

}
```

   Next, we'll need to bind input from the OUYA controller to the script so that it can toggle the paused state.

7. Import the `OuyaInput.cs` script from *Chapter 4, Moving Your Player with Controller Input*, to enable the controller input beyond the inherent touch functionality.

8. Add a call to your `Update` function that updates the controller API for every frame:

```
void Update()
{
  OuyaInput.UpdateControllers();
}
```

9. Add the following logic to call a `ToggleGUI` function whenever the OUYA system button is pressed:

```
void Update()
{
  OuyaInput.UpdateControllers();

  if(OuyaInput.GetButton(OuyaButton.SYSTEM, OuyaPlayer.P01))
  {
    ToggleGUI();
  }
}
```

10. Add a definition for `ToggleGUI` in your `PauseScreen` script as follows:

```
void ToggleGUI()
{

}
```

11. Add an `if/else` statement to either display or hide the **GUI Texture** component based on the state of your `isPaused` variable as shown in the following code:

```
void ToggleGUI()
{
  if(isPaused == false)
  {
    guiTexture.enabled = true;
  }
  else
  {
    guiTexture.enabled = false;
  }
}
```

12. Add a line at the end of `ToggleGUI` that switches the `isPaused` boolean to the opposite value:

```
void ToggleGUI()
{
  if(isPaused == false)
  {
```

```
        guiTexture.enabled = true;
    }
    else
    {
        guiTexture.enabled = false;
    }

    isPaused = !isPaused;
}
```

Now is a good time to check and make sure that this basic toggling functionality works before we add a button. However, we don't want our pause screen to start by default, so first we'll deactivate it.

13. Click the checkbox next to the **GUITexture** component in the `PauseManager` object's **Inspector** window to disable it by default until it is enabled by our script.

Your `PauseManager` object should now look something similar to the following screenshot in the **Inspector** window:

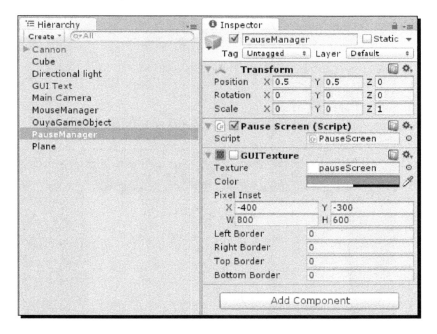

14. Build your game in the OUYA, and make sure that the pause screen can be toggled on and off using the OUYA's system button in the center of the controller.

Now that the pause screen is set up, we'll add a button to it to buy the game.

15. Add a definition to extend Unity's `OnGUI` function in your `PauseScreen` script:

```
void OnGUI()
{

}
```

16. Insert an early return that exits the function if the pause screen isn't active as follows:

```
void OnGUI()
{
  if(!isPaused)
    return;
}
```

17. Add the following lines to your `OnGUI` function to draw a button that will let the player purchase the game:

```
void OnGUI()
{
  if(!isPaused)
    return;

  if(GUI.Button(new Rect(Screen.width / 2 - 50, Screen.height /
    2 - 25, 100, 50), "Buy Full Game"))
  {
    //button functionality goes here
  }
}
```

Your active pause screen should now look similar to the following screenshot:

What just happened?

You've successfully created a toggle able pause screen that contains a button that your player will be able to use to purchase the entitlement product that corresponds to your full game unlock. Everything is finally ready for you to insert your product into the game, so in the next section we'll be adding code that interacts with the product list that you edited in the developer portal.

Time for action – creating your first purchase function

The first step when integrating purchases is to mark any script that manages purchasing as a purchase listener. This tells the OUYA SDK that it will be handling at least one transaction and needs to be able to access the product list. Perform the following steps to create a function for purchasing:

1. Add the following lines of code to your class definition to enable it to listen for all IAP activity:

```
public class PauseScreen :    MonoBehavior,
                              OuyaSDK.IPauseListener,
                              OuyaSDK.IResumeListener,
                              OuyaSDK.IFetchGamerInfoListener,
                              OuyaSDK.IGetProductsListener,
                              OuyaSDK.IPurchaseListener,
                              OuyaSDK.IGetReceiptsListener
{
  ...
}
```

2. Add the following extension to your `PauseScreen` script's `Awake` function to mark it as a listener for all of the previous events:

```
void Awake ()
{
  OuyaSDK.registerFetchGamerInfoListener(this);
  OuyaSDK.registerGetProductsListener(this);
  OuyaSDK.registerPurchaseListener(this);
  OuyaSDK.registerGetReceiptsListener(this);
}
```

It's also good to unregister the object as soon as it's destroyed so that the SDK knows we're done with it. Conveniently, the Unity engine contains a built-in `OnDestroy` function that we can extend to implement the unregistration code.

3. Add the following definition to extend Unity's `OnDestroy` function:

```
void OnDestroy()
{
  OuyaSDK.unregisterFetchGamerInfoListener(this);
  OuyaSDK.unregisterGetProductsListener(this);
  OuyaSDK.unregisterPurchaseListener(this);
  OuyaSDK.unregisterGetReceiptsListener(this);
}
```

Adding these interfaces to our script requires us to implement some mandatory functionality. First of all, we need to create a new line that tells Unity to include generic lists in our compilation.

4. Add the following `using` directive at the top of your `PauseScreen` script:

```
using UnityEngine;
using System.Collections;
using System.Collections.Generic;
```

Next, we need to add definitions for several required functions. Don't worry about filling in the implementations for now; we'll add the functionality to the callbacks when needed.

5. Add definitions for the following functions to your script, with a return type of `void` for all of them:

- `OuyaFetchGamerInfoOnSuccess(string uuid, string username)`
- `OuyaFetchGamerInfoOnFailure(int errorCode, string errorMessage)`
- `OuyaFetchGamerInfoOnCancel()`
- `OuyaGetProductsOnSuccess(List<OuyaSDK.Product> products)`
- `OuyaGetProductsOnFailure(int errorCode, string errorMessage)`
- `OuyaGetProductsOnCancel()`
- `OuyaPurchaseOnSuccess(OuyaSDK.Product product)`
- `OuyaPurchaseOnFailure(int errorCode, string errorMessage)`
- `OuyaPurchaseOnCancel()`
- `OuyaGetReceiptsOnSuccess(List<OuyaSDK.Receipt> receipts)`
- `OuyaGetReceiptsOnFailure(int errorCode, string errorMessage)`
- `OuyaGetReceiptsOnCancel()`

Now that our script is a proper listener, we can interact with products by querying the marketplace. However, we don't want to query the marketplace before in-app purchasing has finished loading, so we'll add a `boolean` flag to keep track of its current status.

6. Declare the following variable after your `isPaused` variable:

```
bool isPaused = false;
bool isIAPReady = false;
```

7. Add the following logic to your `Update` function to manage your `boolean` flag for IAP:

```
void Update()
{
  if(!isIAPReady && OuyaSDK.isIAPInitComplete())
  {
    isIAPReady = true;
  }
}
```

Now we're finally ready to send a purchase attempt whenever the player presses the **Buy Full Game** button.

8. Add the following variable to store the product:

```
bool isPaused = false;
bool isIAPReady = false;
OuyaSDK.Purchasable fullGameUnlock;
```

9. Initialize the variable and assign it a product ID in your `Start` function:

```
void Start()
{
  fullGameUnlock = new OuyaSDK.Purchasable();
  fullGameUnlock.productID = "E_FullGame";
}
```

Make sure that your product ID matches the identifier you set for it on the developer portal.

10. Return to your `OnGUI` function and add the following code to the button functionality region:

```
void OnGUI()
{
  if(!isPaused)
    return;
```

```
        if(GUI.Button(new Rect(Screen.width / 2 - 50, Screen.height /
        2 - 25, 100, 50), "Buy Full Game"))
    {
        //button functionality goes here
        if(isIAPReady)
        {
            OuyaSDK.requestPurchase(fullGameUnlock);
        }
    }
}
```

Our button now sends a purchase request to the marketplace, and we can handle all of the different outcomes from that request using the callback functions we defined earlier.

Callback functions can contain any sort of code you want, and they're useful for performing a certain set of actions whenever a predefined event occurs. For instance, if you want to display a "thank you" message after your player buys a product, you could add in GUI texture code to the OuyaPurchaseOnSuccess function.

You can also store and interact with the data that's passed into the callback function as a parameter. Be careful though, because if the function is triggered by an event that can't pass the proper data or the callback can't handle the data that it is passed, your game will trigger an error. To avoid this, write code to check whether your parameter variables are valid before directly interacting with them.

What just happened?

You've fully equipped a script to handle any kind of IAP operation your user can throw at it. The implementation of IAP can be tricky, especially considering how many configuration steps there are, which include:

◆ Adding listener interfaces to your class definition

◆ Defining callback functions for each listener

◆ Registering and unregistering the script as a listener

◆ Checking to make sure IAP has been initialized before any actions

◆ Including System.Collections.Generic at the top of your script

◆ Creating a Purchasable variable and using it to request a purchase

Have a go hero – initializing product variables dynamically

While your IAP code is now perfectly functional and acceptable, it's considered best practice to load the names and identifiers of your products dynamically so that they can be changed on the developer portal without necessitating any changes to the code base.

Right now, your `Purchasable` variable is hardcoded, meaning that if you changed the identifier in the developer portal, you would need to retype the `productID` variable assignment in your code. Instead of explicitly declaring the product, use the `requestProductList` function to get a collection of every product in your game, and then read the product ID from each element in the list to determine the `Purchasable` variables that you can send to `requestPurchase`.

Time for action – saving and loading successful purchases

As entitlements such as full game unlocks are only purchased once and are expected to be part of a game forever, we need to save the record of our purchase when it's made and check if it exists every time the game is booted up. This is where we'll make use of the OUYA storage API that we mentioned in *Chapter 6, Saving Data to Create Longer Games*, because the data stored in it can exist even after the game is uninstalled and reinstalled. This way, a full game will still be unlocked even on a second installation. Perform the following steps to save and load successful purchases:

1. Add the following lines to your `OuyaPurchaseOnSuccess` callback function to store a value for the passed-in product:

```
public void OuyaPurchaseOnSuccess(OuyaSDK.Product product)
{
  OuyaSDK.OuyaJava.JavaPutGameData(product.name,
    product.identifier);
}
```

   We used two properties of the product variable, the name and the identifier, to set the key and value of the data, respectively. This means that when we're checking whether it already exists, we can simply pass in any product name to `OuyaJavaGetData` and compare the return value to the identifier of that same product.

   We've taken care of saving the data, so next we'll create some code to load this data. This code should verify the state of a purchase right when the game is loaded so that the game loads all of the content that the player is entitled to. We can check this data in two different ways depending on whether the OUYA is connected to the network.

   Ideally, every OUYA is connected to the marketplace using whatever method they used to download the game originally, so first we'll attempt to check the data with an Internet connection.

2. Define a new function called `LoadPreviousPurchases` as shown:

```
void LoadPreviousPurchases()
{

}
```

Our `LoadPreviousPurchases` function will attempt to get a list of receipts of the previously purchased products from the marketplace.

3. Add the following line to the `LoadPreviousPurchases` to retrieve a list of receipts:

```
void LoadPreviousPurchases()
{
        OuyaSDK.requestReceiptList();
}
```

The next step is to expand our successful callback function to loop through our receipts and check if our full game unlock is in any of them.

4. Add the following lines to the `OuyaGetReceiptsOnSuccess` function to iterate through each returned receipt:

```
public void OuyaGetReceiptsOnSuccess(List<OuyaSDK.Receipt>
receipts)
{
  foreach(OuyaSDK.Receipt receipt in receipts)
  {

  }
}
```

5. Add the following lines to your `foreach` statement to check each receipt identifier against the ID of your `Purchasable` object:

```
public void OuyaGetReceiptsOnSuccess(List<OuyaSDK.Receipt>
receipts)
{
  foreach(OuyaSDK.Receipt receipt in receipts)
  {
    if(receipt.identifier == fullGameUnlock.productID)
    {
      //purchase exists
    }
  }
}
```

Now we can tell when the purchase exists, so we'll create a new `boolean` value that will reflect the lock state of the full game.

6. Add the following variable, `isGameUnlocked`, to your `boolean` values:

```
bool isPaused = false;
bool isIAPReady = false;
public static bool isGameUnlocked = false;
```

We marked this value as static because we'll want to access it easily from several different scripts.

7. Add a line to your `OuyaGetReceiptsOnSuccess` function that marks `isGameUnlocked` as `true` after finding a matching full game unlock receipt:

```
public void OuyaGetReceiptsOnSuccess (List<OuyaSDK.Receipt>
receipts)
{
  foreach(OuyaSDK.Receipt receipt in receipts)
  {
    if(receipt.identifier == fullGameUnlock.productID)
    {
      //purchase exists
      isGameUnlocked = true;
    }
  }
}
```

Our game now checks the unlocked state of the game against the list of receipts, but what happens if the receipts can't be fetched due to a lack of connection or any other reason? We need to add functionality to the `OuyaGetReceiptsOnFailure` as well.

8. Add the following lines to the `OuyaGetReceiptsOnFailure` callback to check if our game has been marked as unlocked in storage:

```
public void OuyaGetReceiptsOnFailure(int errorCode, string
errorMessage)
{
  if(fullGameUnlock.identifier ==
    OuyaSDK.OuyaJava.getGameData(fullGameUnlock.name))
  {
    //purchase exists
    isGameUnlocked = true;
  }
}
```

What just happened?

You now have functions that can verify the state of a game irrespective of whether the OUYA is connected to the Internet, thereby ensuring that your players get the full functionality that they paid for even if they're "off the grid."

To extend this functionality further, you can explicitly set the isGameUnlocked variable to false if the console is connected to the Internet and can't find the proper receipt. This will prevent hackers from inserting data into OUYA's local storage and tricking it into thinking they've unlocked the full game.

You can also store unlockables per-account using Unity's PlayerPrefs functionality that we used in *Chapter 6*, *Saving Data to Create Longer Games*. The OUYA storage API stores data per-app instead of per-account, so if you want to differentiate the unlockable functionality between accounts on the same OUYA, you'll have to use a combination of the storage API and PlayerPrefs.

Time for action – reflecting unlocked functionality in games

Coding in-app purchasing can be intimidating because it requires tricky code and doesn't allow for a lot of visual creation in the Unity editor, but at this point, the hardest part is behind you. Now, you get to create a functionality in your game that only gets called if the game is unlocked, and what you add to the full version of your game is completely up to you.

In this section, we'll add a different, special cannonball to our prototype that bounces on impact instead of landing firmly. Any user who has unlocked the full game will be able to fire this new type of cannonball in place of the standard one. Perform the following steps to display the unlocked functionality:

1. Create a new prefab called CannonballSpecial in your Prefabs folder.

2. Create a primitive sphere using the **Create** menu in the **Hierarchy** window and link it to your new prefab.

3. Create a new, unique material called CannonballSpecialMat in your Materials folder.

4. Import the **Physic Materials** package from the **Asset** menu and attach the **Bouncy** material to the **Sphere Collider** component of your CannonballSpecial prefab.

Your prefab should now look similar to the following screenshot in the **Inspector** window:

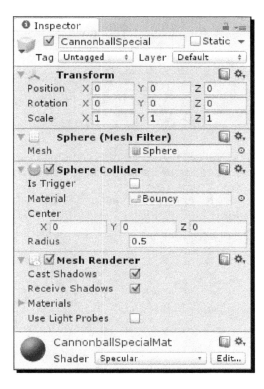

The only thing our prefab is still missing is a component that will make it affected by gravity.

5. Add a **Rigidbody** component to the `CannonballSpecial` prefab so that it's treated like a physical object as soon as we instantiate it.

Next, we'll turn to our code to incorporate the new cannonball into our existing functions.

6. Open `CannonScript.cs` and declare the following new variable after the original cannonball prefab:

```
public GameObject cannonballPrefab;
public GameObject cannonballSpecialPrefab;
```

7. Link the `CannonballSpecial` prefab to your new variable by dragging it into the new field in the `Cannon` prefab's **Inspector** window.

The new **Cannon Script** component on the `Cannon` prefab should now look similar to following screenshot in the **Inspector** window:

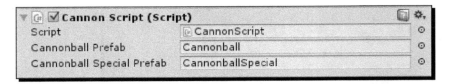

Next, we'll add some logic around the actual cannonball instantiation to pick an appropriate cannonball to fire based on the lock state of the game.

8. Add the following lines to replace your cannonball instantiation in the `FireCannon` functions:

```
void FireCannon(float xForce, float yForce)
{
    ...
    GameObject newCannonball;

    if(PauseScreen.isGameUnlocked)
    {
        newCannonball =
        (GameObject)Instantiate(cannonballSpecialPrefab,
            cannonballPos, Quaternion.identity);
    }
    else
    {
        newCannonball = (GameObject)Instantiate(cannonballPrefab,
            cannonballPos, Quaternion.identity);
    }
    ...
}
```

9. Test your new functionality with the game unlocked, either by setting `isGameUnlocked` to `true` manually in code or by building to the OUYA and attempting to purchase it in-game.

 Don't worry about needing to spend money to test your in-app purchases; all purchases are free if you're using the same account that the game is registered under. However, if you have two separate accounts for developing and playing, make sure you're using the one for developing before attempting the purchase.

What just happened?

You've provided an upgraded base mechanic to your players that have unlocked the full game, which is the most simple and straightforward way to demonstrate the difference in-app purchases can make.

The more functionality you add to a product, the more likely your players are to buy it. Making a bouncy cannonball that's more likely to hit your target is a good start, but think about all of the different areas you could expand on in the full version of the game.

Adding polish with Unity Asset Store packages

In this section, we'll learn how to add a visual effect to your cannonball so that it enhances the visual complexity as well as the mechanical complexity.

Time for action – adding explosions to your cannonballs

What's a game without a few good explosions, right? You can make your cannon game much more visually appealing by adding some explosion effects to the special cannonballs. Making your own explosion effects can be tricky and time-consuming, but fortunately, there's a package on Unity Asset Store called **Detonator** that allows you to use basic pre-built explosion prefabs for free. Perform the following steps to add explosions:

1. Open the **Window** menu on Unity's toolbar and click on **Asset Store** to open the **Asset Store** window.

2. Sign in with your Unity account (or create one if you don't have one yet) to display the storefront.

Unity Asset Store features several handy packages and tools for building features outside of your own skill range. The store features code, art assets, editor tools and more, as shown in the following screenshot:

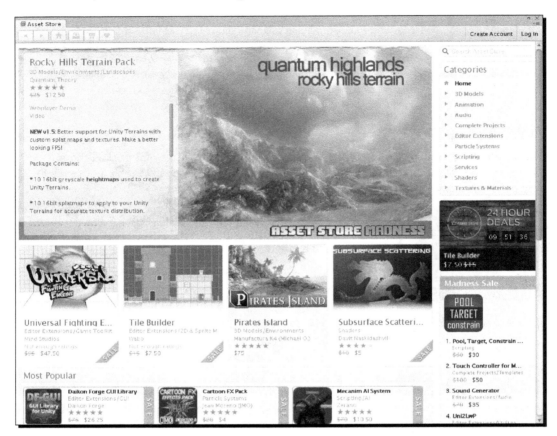

3. Type Detonator into the search bar in the upper-right corner of the **Asset Store** window.

4. Click on the package labeled **Detonator Explosion Framework** on the search results page to be taken to the store page for it, where you will see a **Download** button.

5. Click on **Download** to begin downloading the packaged files. As soon as the process has completed, Unity will automatically display an **Import** dialog for all of the new items.

6. Import the entire framework and close the **Asset Store** window.

Now we're ready to add one of the explosion prefabs to our special cannonball, but first we have to decide when it will explode. Making it explode as soon as it touches any surface will negate the bouncing functionality we coded, so we'll make a script that causes the cannonball to explode after a certain number of bounces instead.

7. Create a new script called `CannonballSpecial.cs` and open it in your code editor.

8. Add the following variable to track the number of times the cannonball bounces:

```
private int numBounces = 0;
```

9. Add a definition to extend Unity's `OnCollisionEnter` functionality where we will capture the bounces:

```
void OnCollisionEnter(Collision collidingObj)
{

}
```

10. Add the following line to increment the number of bounces every time the cannonball enters a collision:

```
void OnCollisionEnter(Collision collidingObj)
{
    numBounces++;
}
```

11. Attach the `CannonballSpecial` script to your `CannonballSpecial` prefab.

12. Add a new `GameObject` variable to the script to hold the explosion prefab that we're going to use:

```
private int numBounces = 0;
public GameObject explosionPrefab;
```

13. Link the `Detonator-Simple` prefab from the `Detonator Explosion Framework` folder to the **Explosion Prefab** field in the `CannonballSpecial` prefab's **Inspector** window.

The **Cannonball Special** script component on your `CannonballSpecial` prefab should now look similar to the following screenshot in the **Inspector** window:

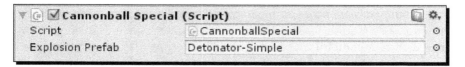

14. Add the following lines to the `CannonballSpecial` script's `OnCollisionEnter` function to make it instantiate an explosion and then destroy itself after two bounces:

```
void OnCollisionEnter(Collision collidingObj)
{
  numBounces++;

  if(numBounces > 2)
  {
    Instantiate(explosionPrefab, transform.position,
      transform.rotation);
    Destroy(this.gameObject);
  }
}
```

15. Test your new code and watch as your special cannonballs bounce twice and then explode.

Your explosion will look similar to the one shown in the following screenshot:

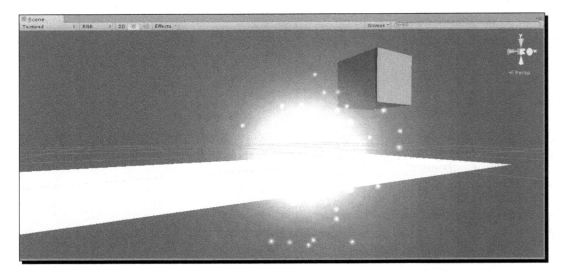

What just happened?

Your special cannonballs are now accompanied by a satisfying boom whenever they explode; another example of a feature available to people who unlock the full version of your game. Get creative with your content! Make sure to add interesting features to attract the attention of free players, but don't be afraid to add some shock-and-awe functionalities to thank your paying players for their support.

You learned how to use Unity Asset Store in this section as well, which is an invaluable tool for developers to explore new ideas and download or purchase functionality that their fellow developers have created solely for the purpose of selling in a package. Who knows, maybe one day you'll be creating assets on the asset store yourself!

Pricing your in-app purchases

Pricing is a tough subject in game development. How do you put a concrete price on various elements of your hard work? Triple-A games typically stay close to a standard pricing, but when it comes to indie titles (and especially in-game content packs), pricing is entirely up to the developer.

There's no right answer to how much you should charge for your game, but here are a few tips to get you started.

Setting the price of your full game

When you're deciding how much it will cost your players to unlock the full game or any new DLC packages, there are a few aspects you should consider. These are complexity, length, and replay value, described as follows:

◆ **Complexity**: At some level, the work that you put into your game should be reflected in its price. This doesn't necessarily mean front-facing complexity but is more about the time and effort it took to create the game. You can usually sell a three-dimensional game for more than a two-dimensional game, charge more for a game that includes realistic physics simulations, and up the price for each additional mode that your game offers.

◆ **Length**: The price your player pays for your game should give them a proportional amount of expected play time. For instance, no matter how good your game is, it would be unreasonable to charge $10 for 10 minutes of play. It's a good idea to play through some games fully and note how long it takes to explore every facet of each before comparing their prices. Again, there's no set standard that links gameplay length and price, but use your best judgment to find a happy medium that's feasible for your audience and still earns you some money for your work.

◆ **Replay value**: Your game doesn't necessarily have to have a long story or extensive progression to garner a lot of play time. Some games keep players coming back with replay value, or the desire of the player to repeat the same level/procedure over and over. In *Chapter 1, Experiencing the OUYA*, you played *Canabalt*, which is an endless runner game built on replay value; the mechanics never change and the environments remain basically the same, but the player is expected to play several times to try to get the top score.

Replay value is commonly high in games that feature the multiplayer functionality, such as *Towerfall*. Note in the following screenshot how the level is simple enough to fit on one screen without panning, but it's replay value is high because pitting a player against another player is almost certain to create a unique experience every time.

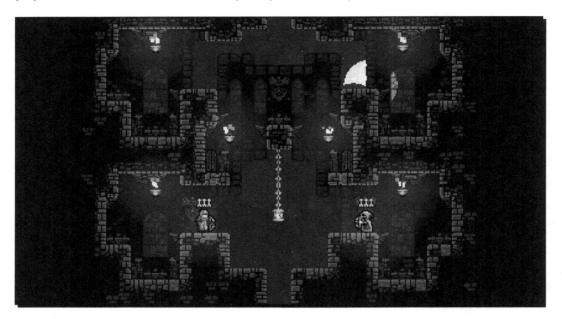

Picking a monetization model

Just as there are two different kinds of products that you can sell in your OUYA game, there are two main monetization models that you can choose from to structure your in-app purchases: paygate and free-to-play. Both of these models focus primarily on one product type or the other, and they can make a big difference depending on the experience you're trying to convey. They are described as follows:

◆ **Paygate**: The paygate model is centered around the idea of a full game unlock entitlement. As the name implies, the player is met with a "gate" or "wall" after playing the game for a short time that asks them if they want to pay to unlock the full game. If they pay, the rest of the game is immediately unlocked. Payment isn't required, so players don't have to spend money on a game they don't enjoy, but if they don't pay, they are limited to the functionality of the introductory stages. Further functionality may be added to the game with entitlement products that represent the DLC content. Despite a strong focus on entitlement products, a game made under the paygate model can also feature consumables, such as potions and weapons, as long as they're still applicable to players who may own the full game but not any DLC.

- **Free-to-play**: Free-to-play games are built on the condition that it's possible to experience the full game without paying a cent. Consumables are typically abundant in free-to-play games but none are required to add functionality to the game; they only make certain aspects of the game quicker or easier for purchasing players. While games under the paygate model can use consumables, games under the free-to-play model can't really make use of entitlements because they create a major disconnect between paying and non-paying players. It's important to avoid neglecting your free players because even if they don't spend as much money as other players, a positive experience will still help your game spread from them to all of their potentially paying friends. *Guns'n'Glory*, one of the games we looked at earlier in this chapter, is a free-to-play game. The game features several consumables to purchase, but their sole function is to immediately pay out a certain amount of in-game currency to the player, which a free player could easily earn by playing and avoid having to pay.

Beware of an imbalance of power between non-paying players and paying players in your multiplayer games. You may want to remove paid power-ups in your multiplayer mode all together, or test them extensively to ensure players cannot gain the upper hand over their opponents using money alone. Nobody likes a pay-to-win game.

Have a go hero – tying it all together with more products

Use everything you've learned about in-app purchases in this chapter to create at least two more products that change your game. As we've been working with entitlements, try creating a consumable; they're processed the same way in code but their utility and philosophy differs greatly (make sure you brush up on the monetization models for a good guideline). The following are some ideas of functionality that you can add with in-app purchases in your cannonball game:

- A cannonball that splits off into several others
    - Use the logic you used to instantiate an explosion and instead instantiate several new cannonballs
    - Apply semi-random velocity to the child cannonballs to create a widespread yet inaccurate buckshot effect

Try adding a call to `GameObject.Instantiate` in an extension of the cannonball's `OnDestroy` function.

- ◆ A cannonball that doesn't fall as quickly for more precise shots
    - ❑ Edit the mass values of this cannonball's `Rigidbody` component to drastically change the effect gravity has on it

 The mass property can be viewed and changed in the cannonball prefab's **Inspector** window. Try changing it in the middle of a game to see how different values affect the cannonballs.

- ◆ A consumable item that makes the next 10 cannonballs you fire twice the default size
    - ❑ Keep an integer variable of how many special shots the user has remaining
    - ❑ Double the scale value for each special shot and display a GUI message when the player runs out of special shots

 If the consumable item is active and the user still has special shots, call the `transform.Scale` function from the `Start` function of the cannonball script.

The only limit to your in-app purchases is your imagination. Add in several independent packages so that your players can pay what they want for the features they enjoy without having to spend too much on features that they don't want included.

Pop quiz – talking shop

Q1. Which of the following categories of a product are most common in games that follow the "paygate" monetization model?

1. Entitlements
2. Consumables
3. Both

Q2. Which of the following categories of a product are most common in games that follow the "free-to-play" monetization model?

1. Entitlements
2. Consumables
3. Both

Q3. What property of a `Purchasable` object is used to access the corresponding item from the OUYA developer portal?

1. Name

2. Key

3. Identifier

Summary

In this chapter, you learned all the steps involved in expanding a game with in-app purchases. In-app purchases enable you to make your game more complex with an additional functionality such as letting players pick new mechanics à la carte and providing one-time-use items to get players out of a tough spot or to the next level more quickly.

You also learned about Unity Asset Store, accessible through the **Window** menu in Unity. The asset store is a community-driven site where developers can upload packaged Unity tools, either for free or for a price. If you ever want to implement new mechanics that you don't have any experience with and you don't know where to start, Unity Asset Store is a good jumping-off point.

Now that you've had a chance to experience every element your games can contain, we'll discuss packaging your final games and preparing them for deployment on the OUYA marketplace in the next chapter.

8
Polishing and Prepping Your Game for Deployment

You now have the knowledge and the code base to create any game and make it run smoothly. In the previous chapter, Chapter 7, Expanding Your Gameplay with In-App Purchases, you learned how to add in-app purchasing to your projects, allowing your players to explore additional content in your games and unlock advanced features.

In this chapter, we'll shift our focus from project fundamentals to several different polishing techniques that you can use to make your game stand out. In addition to being clean and polished, your game also has to meet the OUYA content guidelines before it can be submitted to the marketplace. We'll review the steps to create an acceptable submission in this chapter as well.

Here's a summary of what we'll cover:

- ◆ Meeting the OUYA content guidelines
- ◆ Polishing your aesthetic and mechanics
- ◆ Packaging your project for submission

Above all, we want to ensure all of the final changes we make adhere to the content guidelines, so the first thing we'll do is prepare a game for marketplace submission using the marble coin prototype as an example. If you've been working on your own game independent of these tutorials, feel free to follow along using that instead of the marble coin prototype; these steps can be applied to any project.

Meeting the OUYA content guidelines

The power to produce and potentially publish a game is entirely in the hands of the OUYA audience, but the OUYA team must approve any submitted game before it's published on the marketplace. To ensure quality games and a uniform review process, a list of content guidelines is available that includes all of the recommended and required criteria for your OUYA projects. You can find the latest version of this list at https://devs.ouya.tv/developers/docs/content-review-guidelines.

Time for action – containing game elements within the safe zone

The OUYA console works on any TV or monitor with a **High-Definition Multimedia Interface** (**HDMI**) port, so you can expect your game to be played on a lot of different screens. Certain screens can experience overscan, which cuts off the outer border of the screen and can potentially hide game elements that are right on the edge of the window.

 Overscan is the result of TV and monitor manufacturers cropping the screen to ensure that there are no blank borders or visible edges. However, because overscan is different on each screen, it can cut off parts of what you're viewing as well. To minimize overscan, try setting your monitor to a 1:1 pixel ratio (methods of doing this vary, but can be found in the manual of your TV or monitor).

To make sure everything in your game is visible no matter what screen it's being played on, OUYA features a toggleable "safe zone" that highlights the area that should contain vital game elements. Safe zones vary by TV but are usually between 80 and 90 percent of the screen space. We'll use this safe zone to make sure everything important is where it ideally should be.

We'll begin by enabling a developer overlay that allows us to visualize the safe zone. Perform the following steps to do so:

1. Connect your OUYA console to your computer via its included **Universal Serial Bus** (**USB**) cable.

2. Open a command-line window (Terminal if you're using Mac OS X, Command Prompt if you're using Windows).

3. Run the `adb devices` command to ensure that your OUYA console is connected and ready. OUYA will appear as a series of numbers and letters on the device list, similar to the following screenshot:

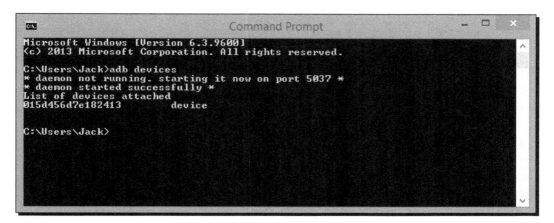

If your console does not show up in the list of attached devices, you may need to run the `adb kill-server` command and then run `adb devices` again. This will restart the `adb` service before fetching the list of devices, and it's a good thing to try before troubleshooting your physical connections.

4. Start your marble game on OUYA. This can be done by clicking on **Build & Run** in Unity's **File** menu, or if you've tested it on OUYA recently, you can start it from the console in the **Play** menu.

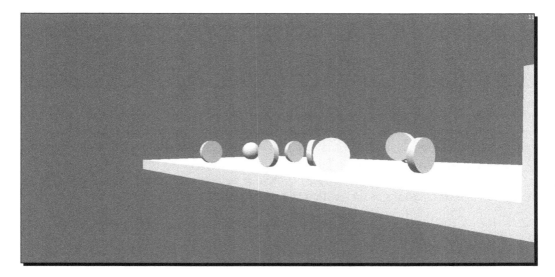

5. Return to the command-line window on your computer while the game is still running and enter the following commands:

```
adb shell
su
```

These two commands will open a shell that can interact directly with OUYA and give it root permissions, which are needed to display the safe zone.

6. Run the following command to toggle the safe zone display over your marble game:

```
am start -n
   tv.ouya.console/tv.ouya.console.launcher.ToggleSafeZoneActivity
```

The display will appear directly on top of the normal game view, as shown in the following screenshot:

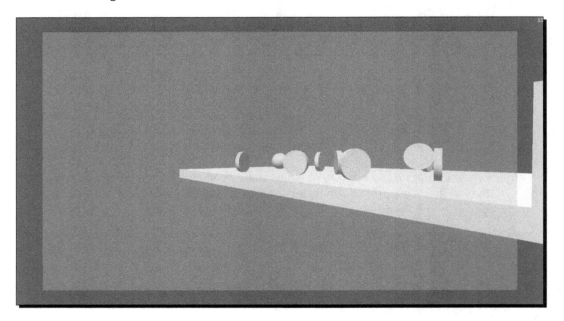

The transparent green overlay that appears on top of your game is the safe zone, and everything important to the user must be within that box. Already, we can see in the previous screenshot that our GUI element, situated in the upper-left corner, is outside the safe zone and far too small for the monitor's resolution (1920 x 1080). The safe zone will typically display over your default resolution, but you can test on smaller resolutions as well with a simple command.

7. Enter the following command in the command line to test your game on a 1280 x 720 resolution:

```
am display-size 1280x720
```

The screen will adjust your game to display in a smaller resolution and fill the rest of the screen with black, as shown in the following screenshot:

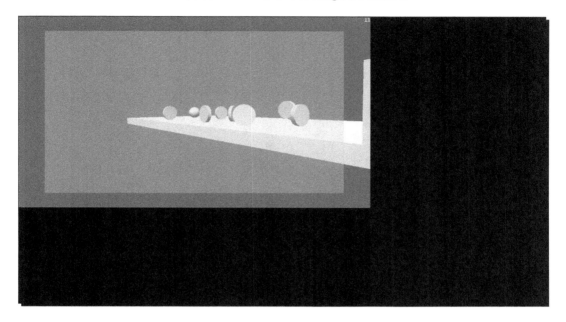

The font size is slightly easier to read on a smaller resolution, but it's still far outside the safe zone, so we'll have to change our GUI text to meet the OUYA content guidelines.

8. Select the **GUI Text** object in your hierarchy to display its properties in the **Inspector** window.

9. Increase the font size from `20` to `50` in the **Inspector** window.

10. Change the position of the **GUI Text** object from `1.0, 1.0, 0.0` to `0.95, 0.95, 0.0`.

Now that the text is more easily visible and farther from the edge of the screen, we can check the safe zone again.

11. Click on the **Build & Run** option in Unity's **File** menu to deploy your latest build to the console.

12. If the safe zone isn't enabled already, toggle it on and ensure that the text lies completely within the bounds of the safe zone.

We now know that our GUI element will be visible on any screen because it fits within the safe zone overlay, as shown in the following screenshot:

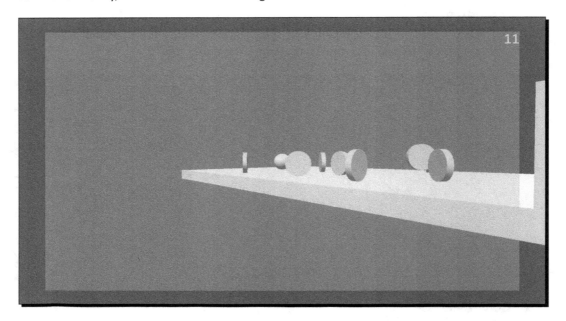

Note that the GUI element is now large enough to easily read without interfering with the game area and the text is within the safe zone, which guarantees that it will be visible on any TV that supports OUYA.

What just happened?

You just learned how to toggle the safe zone reference and then tweak a visual element to fit within the safe zone, which is crucial to ensure the playability of your game across any model of television or monitor. You also learned how to change the display resolution of OUYA on your own monitor using the command line, so you can test multiple resolutions without needing multiple screens.

Some game developers measure their safe zones and then cover anything outside of the safe zone in screen-safe tape, so they never forget to stay inside of it. This isn't mandatory, but at the very least, you'll have to make a final check before submitting your game to ensure that the screen specifications fit the OUYA content guidelines.

Time for action – creating icons for your game

Up until this point, the icon for your game has been shown on OUYA's **Play** menu as a standard Unity icon. Before submitting your game, it needs to have a unique icon that will draw attention to it and differentiate it from other games on the market, so we'll now create a set of custom icons by performing the following steps:

1. Open the folder that contains your `RollingMarble` project and navigate to `RollingMarble\Assets\Plugins\Android\res`.

2. Open the folder named `drawable` and examine the file inside it named `app_icon.png`.

   The `app_icon.png` file is the icon that will appear when people view your app from the OUYA marketplace. Note that this is different from the icon that will appear on the **Play** menu; this is the one that most people will see before they download the game.

3. Use your preferred image manipulation program to make yourself an app icon. Get creative! You can have anything in your app icon as long as it's appropriate for all ages and it fits the required resolution of 96 x 96.

4. Once you finish creating your custom icon, save it over the old icon in the same folder with the same name.

5. Next, you'll change your game's OUYA icon. This is the large rectangular icon that shows up in the OUYA menu.

6. Navigate back to `RollingMarble\Assets\Plugins\Android\res` and open the folder named `drawable-xhdpi`.

7. Create your own custom OUYA icon to be displayed in the OUYA **Play** menu. The requirements are the same as the app icon, but with a resolution of 732 x 412.

8. Save the icon over the old one with the same name.

9. Click on **Build & Run** again to deploy your new package to the console.

10. Double-click on the OUYA system button to return to the **Play** menu and see your new icon.

The icon will also be visible in the main menu as your most recently played title, as shown in the following screenshot:

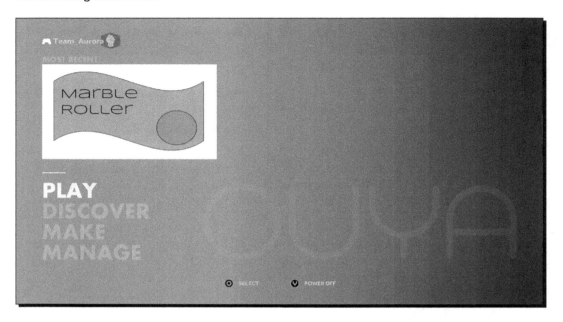

What just happened?

When you changed the icon images in the res folder within your Unity project, it replaced the images that Unity uses to package your game into its APK file. Each game on the OUYA marketplace needs to have its own icon, and the small app icon and the larger OUYA icon are great tools to help you make your game stand out.

Following the Unity Submission Checklist

In addition to the safe zone requirements, there are several technical criteria that your game must meet in order to be accepted. These criteria include, but are not limited to, the following:

- The game displays properly on 720dpi and 1080dpi
- The game must be playable offline
- The user must be able to easily figure out how to play
- The game cannot experience crashes or major gameplay bugs

While you're finalizing your game, it's a good idea to follow the full Submission Checklist, which can be downloaded from the Games page on the OUYA developer portal. This extensive checklist contains every requirement that games must meet to be accepted and includes several recommended features as well.

Now that you've polished your game's packaging, we'll focus on some advanced techniques for polishing the actual content. If you're working on your own project and don't feel the need to add anything more to it, you can skip right to the final *Time for action – creating your game on the developer portal* section—all of the following tutorials until the final one are assorted polishing techniques that you can experiment with at any time.

Polishing Unity projects in depth

This section will focus on several of the finer points of what makes up any game, including the title screen and end screen, tutorial, camera, and audio. While the scripting you've done so far has mostly focused on game logic and mechanics, the scripts you write in this section will provide your game with a cohesive structure and frame the user experience.

Creating your game flow

The marble game is perfectly playable right now, but there's no introductory title screen to prepare the player or a reset/death screen that appears if they roll off the side of the level. A title screen and end screen are the two ends to your game flow, and you should be able to continue to play the game through the loop regardless of victory or loss.

Time for action – creating a title screen

Your title screen is the first part of your game that your player will see, and it's the first part of the game flow we'll create. The title screen doesn't need much—we just want to present the title to the player and provide a button to start the game. Perform the following steps to create the title screen:

1. Create a new scene called `TitleScreen` in your `RollingMarble` project.
2. Click on the **Main Camera** object in the **Hierarchy** window to select it.

3. Change the **Background** color property to black so that it appears as shown in the following screenshot:

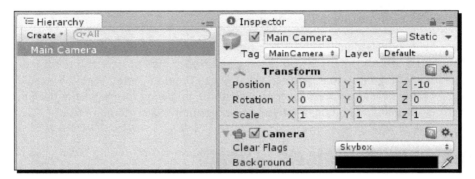

Your title so far is just a flat black screen, so what it needs now is a logo.

4. Using your preferred image manipulator (that is, Paint, Photoshop, or GIMP), create a logo for your game in your preferred size (this tutorial will use a logo approximately 600 pixels wide and 400 pixels tall).

5. Save your logo in a location that you will be able to find easily. As this is the first texture we're applying to our marble project, we should create a folder to hold it and all future textures.

6. Create a folder named Textures in your project's Asset directory.

7. Move the logo that you created into the new Textures folder of your Unity project.

2D images are displayed in Unity using an object type called **GUI Texture**, so we'll have to create one to display our logo. Alternatively, you can make use of one of Unity's core 2D features and drag-and-drop an image directly onto the scene to add it to your game world.

8. Open the **Create** menu in the **Hierarchy** window and select **GUI Texture**. By default, a new **GUI Texture** object will display the Unity logo and name itself UnityWatermark-small in the object hierarchy.

9. Click on the **GUI Texture** object in the hierarchy while it is selected to rename it. Name the object Title Logo.

10. Click-and-drag your texture from the `Textures` folder to the **Texture** property of the **GUI Texture** component of `Title Logo` to set it as the image to display.

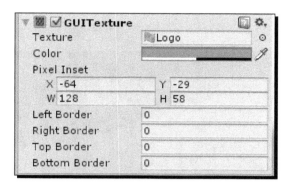

11. You'll notice that your logo is most likely skewed and too small because it is still set to the small Unity watermark's pixel inset. To change this, set the **W** and **H** values to the pixel width and pixel height of your logo, respectively.

The **X** and **Y** values of the **Pixel Inset** property let you set where to draw the origin of the image. Unity's origins are in the upper-right corner of objects by default, but setting a negative inset of half of the width and height will draw it directly in the center. The watermark already had a centered inset, but we need to change it to match the new dimensions of our logo.

12. Set your **Pixel Inset** property's **X** and **Y** values to the negative of half of your logo's width and height, respectively. For instance, if your image is 600 pixels wide and 400 pixels high, set the **X** inset value to -300 and the **Y** inset value to -200.

13. Check your **Game** window to make sure your logo looks like it's positioned and scaled correctly. It should be the correct size and positioned directly in the center of the window.

You can see that the logo is positioned and scaled correctly because it's in the center of the **Game** window and the red circle is not stretched vertically or horizontally, as demonstrated in the following screenshot:

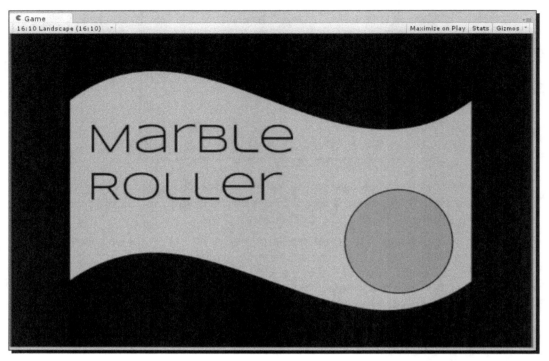

Now that the constraints are set properly, you can move the logo to wherever you want on the screen by editing its **Transform** component. Once you've done that, all you need to do is add a button.

14. Create a new C# script named `StartButton.cs` in your `Code` folder and attach it to the **GUI Text** object.

15. Open `StartButton.cs` in your code editor.

16. Add in a method to extend Unity's `OnGUI` function and add the following lines to it:

```
void OnGUI()
{
  if(GUI.Button(new Rect(Screen.width / 2 - 50, Screen.height /
    2 + 25, 100, 50), "Start"))
  {
    Application.LoadLevel("level1");
  }
}
```

The numbers following the screen width and height variables represent the size of the button in pixels. We subtract `50` from the screen width and add `25` to the height, which are half of the values we used for width and height, respectively; this is to account for the positioning offset and to ensure that the button remains in the very center of the screen.

The `GUI.Button` function we called makes a simple button that displays whatever content you input in dimensions you define, and encapsulating it in an `if` statement allows us to easily handle a button press. In the case of our start button, we want it to load the level that contains our rolling marble, so we use `Application.LoadLevel` to load the `level1` scene (or whatever your main scene is named).

17. Open the **Build Settings** window from Unity's **File** menu and click on **Add Current** to add the title screen to the build and make it accessible from other scenes. Ensure that it is the first item in the list so that it is loaded as soon as the application is started.

As you're changing the first scene, you need to change the position of `OuyaGameObject`. It's already been added to your game scene, but OUYA requires it to be in the first scene that's loaded.

18. Drag an instance of `OuyaGameObject` from your **Project** window into your **TitleScreen** scene.

19. Don't forget to delete `OuyaGameObject` in your game scene, as it is not necessary to be loaded twice.

What just happened?

Your game now begins with a title screen instead of throwing the player directly into the game, which also gives you a place to explain the rules or add paths to other options (we'll learn how to add a game tutorial later in this chapter in the *Creating a tutorial* section).

You used a **GUI Texture** object, which is a type of object that displays any image imported into Unity according to a defined size and pixel inset. You've now used both the **GUI Texture** and **GUI Text** objects, so think about which ones are better to use in different scenarios. Is the information that you're trying to convey to your player a number that they'll want to read or could it be represented as a picture or symbol instead?

You also had your first foray into Unity's built-in GUI system, which features a simple button set up in just a few lines of code. The Unity GUI is quick to set up but features multiple points of customization and advanced coding; if you want to dive further into Unity GUI techniques, check out the GUI scripting guide at `http://docs.unity3d.com/Documentation/Components/GUIScriptingGuide.html`.

Time for action – creating a loss screen

You can already exit the game by winning because we coded a collision with the cube at the other end of the level to result in the win screen being displayed. However, if the player accidentally rolls off the level, there's no way for them to get back up and try again.

To fix this, we'll create a loss screen that lets the user replay the game. The process of building our loss screen will follow our process of building the title screen, but we'll also create a trigger so that the loss screen is displayed when the marble falls off the level. Perform the following steps to create a loss screen:

1. Create a new scene called LossScreen in your RollingMarble project.

2. Set your preferred background color in the **Inspector** window for the **Main Camera** object in the **Hierarchy** window.

3. Create a new **GUI Text** object from the **Create** menu in the **Hierarchy** window.

4. Set the **Text** property of the new **GUI Text** object to read You Lose.

5. Set the font size of the **GUI Text** object to be 50.

6. Set the **Anchor** property of the text to **middle center** and the **Alignment** property to **center**.

7. Set the **GUI Text** object to display in your preferred color by changing the **Color** property.

Once you're finished, you should have something that looks like this:

The only addition left to make in this scene is to add a reset button that returns the user to the title screen.

8. Create a new script called `ResetButton.cs` and attach it to the **GUI Text** object.

9. Open `ResetButton.cs` in your code editor.

10. Add the following extension to `OnGUI` in the `ResetButton.cs` script:

```
void OnGUI()
{
  if(GUI.Button(new Rect(Screen.width / 2 - 50, Screen.height /
    2 + 25, 100, 50), "Reset"))
  {
    Application.LoadLevel("TitleScreen");
  }
}
```

You'll notice that this code is the same basic code we used for the title screen button, but we changed the text of the button to read **Reset** and we told it to load the title screen instead of the game screen.

11. Open the **Build Settings** window from Unity's **File** menu and click on **Add Current** to add the loss screen to the build and make it accessible from other scenes.

The only thing left is to detect when the marble leaves the level, which we'll do by placing an invisible collider underneath the main platform.

12. Double-click on your `level1` scene to open the main game area in your Unity editor.

13. Create a new cube and position it underneath the platform at `0, -7.5, 0`.

14. We want to scale this cube into a platform that will catch the marble whenever it falls off of the main platform, so we'll need to make it relatively large. Increase the **X** scale to `50` and the **Z** scale to `30` so that it looks something like the following screenshot:

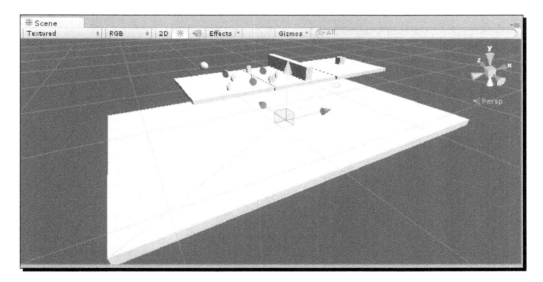

15. We want our lower platform to serve as a trigger but it doesn't need to be visible, so disable the renderer by unchecking the box at the top of the **Mesh Renderer** component window.

16. Check the **Is Trigger** box within the **Box Collider** component of the platform.

Your lower platform should now be an invisible trigger, only highlighted by a green wireframe box whenever it's selected in the object hierarchy.

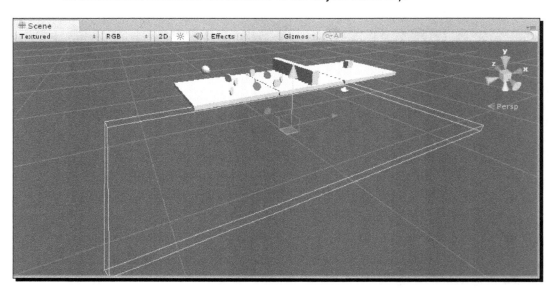

All that's left is to code the collider trigger that will send our player to the loss/reset screen if they fall.

17. Create a new script called `FallPlatform.cs` and attach it to the invisible trigger object.

18. Open `FallPlatform.cs` in your code editor.

19. Add the following extension to `OnTriggerEnter` in the script:

```
void OnTriggerEnter(Collider collider)
{
    Application.LoadLevel("LossScreen");
}
```

20. Test your code by running the game in the Unity editor and rolling the marble off of the platform. When the marble collides with the lower platform, it will activate your `OnTriggerEnter` extension and load the loss screen.

What just happened?

With the addition of a loss screen with a **Replay** button, your game loop is now complete. You added a loss condition that is triggered by an invisible nonphysical collision when the player rolls off the map, which sends the player to a loss screen where they can restart the game and attempt it again.

Your game can now be played as many times as the player wants in one play session, no matter how many times they win or lose. A solid game loop is crucial to a game's functionality, and your title and end screens take some focus away from the main game screen to help to break up the game into a typical beginning, middle, and end.

Creating a tutorial

The OUYA content guidelines require that your player be able to easily figure out how to play, and what better way to do that than with a tutorial. In this section, we'll go through the process of creating a tutorial with text instructions and a sample marble that can be moved around safely to test the controls.

Time for action – creating a tutorial scene

Perform the following steps to create a tutorial scene:

1. Create a new scene called `TutorialScreen` in your `RollingMarble` project.

2. Create a cube primitive and position it at `0, 0, 0`.

3. Scale the cube to `10, 1, 10` so that it's a large enough surface for the player to roll around on.

4. Change the **Y** value of the **Main Camera** to `5` so that it can give the player an elevated view that's easier to observe the marble with.

Your scene should now look something like the following screenshot in the
Scene window:

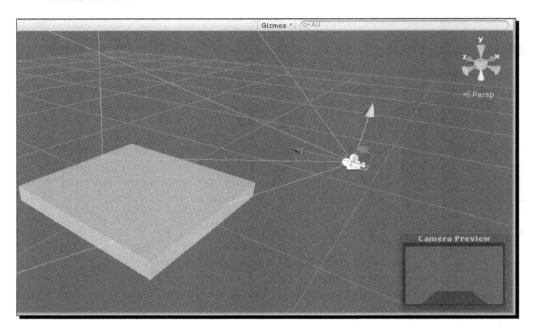

5. We don't want our player to be able to fall off the level and lose on the tutorial screen,
so create four cube primitives and scale them into walls for the platform as shown:

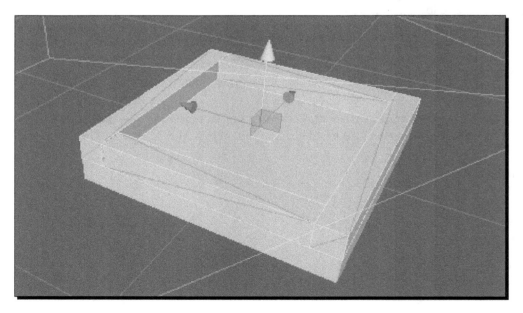

6. The scene looks very dark in the camera preview. Add **Directional Light** by navigating to **Hierarchy| Create** menu with default settings.

7. Click-and-drag an instance of your `Marble` prefab from the **Project** window onto the new platform in your scene.

As you stored all of the properties of the marble in a prefab, no additional coding is necessary to make this marble work in the tutorial—in fact, if you press play right now, you can test the tutorial level by moving the marble around it.

8. The camera doesn't follow the marble yet, so apply the `TrackingCamera.cs` script to the **Main Camera** object in the **Hierarchy** menu.

9. Tell the camera which object to track by clicking-and-dragging the `Marble` object in the **Hierarchy** menu to the **Object To Track** variable field in the **Inspector** menu.

You've now got a good "sandbox" area for your player to get used to the controls of the game before reaching any objectives or pitfalls, but it could still use some explanatory text elements.

10. Create three new **GUI Text** objects and position them in the upper-right corner of the screen in a list format.

11. Change the text of the GUI elements to reflect the controls of the game. Make sure to color-coordinate each text element with its corresponding face button on the OUYA controller. When you're finished, your game screen should look like the following screenshot:

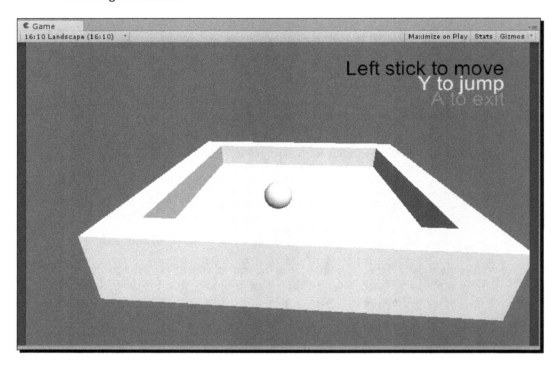

12. Make sure your new GUI elements are inside the safe zone. Build to OUYA and toggle the safe zone display to ensure that the game text still meets the content requirements.

    The only thing left to do in our tutorial is code our exit functionality, which we'll trigger with the *A* button.

13. Create a new script called `TutorialScript.cs` and attach it to the current instance of your marble.

In the past, almost every change you've made has been applied to an object prefab so that the change is automatically applied on every other instance. However, we don't need to handle tutorial exiting when we're not in the tutorial, so in this case, we're only attaching `TutorialScript.cs` to the marble instance in the tutorial scene.

14. Open `TutorialScript.cs` in your code editor and add the following lines of code to the `Update` function:

```
void Update()
{
  if(OuyaInput.GetButton(OuyaButton.A, OuyaPlayer.P01))
  {
    Application.LoadLevel("TitleScreen");
  }
}
```

15. Add the `TutorialScreen` scene to the build by opening the **Build Settings** menu and clicking on **Add Current**.

What just happened?

You've taken your first steps into creating a tutorial for your game. Tutorials can be as simple or as complex as you want them to be; as long as they give a player an understanding of how to navigate your game world, you can convey that understanding in any way you want. This could simply be with a screen with 2D instructions, a more interactive demo like the one we created, or an entire level of the game with a special focus on teaching the player.

Time for action – linking your tutorial to your game

Your tutorial level is ready to play, but we still need a way to access it. We'll accomplish this by adding another button to your title screen directly underneath the start button. Perform the following steps to link the tutorial:

1. Open the scene named `TitleScreen` and double-click on the `StartButton.cs` script to open it in your code editor.

2. Add the following lines of code in your `OnGUI` function to create a tutorial button immediately below the start button:

```
void OnGUI()
{
  if(GUI.Button(new Rect(Screen.width / 2 - 50, Screen.height /
    2 + 25, 100, 50), "Start"))
  {
    Application.LoadLevel("level1");
  }

  //create a tutorial button
  if(GUI.Button(new Rect(Screen.width / 2 - 50, Screen.height /
    2 + 125, 100, 50), "Tutorial"))
  {
```

```
        Application.LoadLevel("TutorialScreen");
    }
}
```

Much like the start and reset buttons, the code for the tutorial button is uniform with the others; we only needed to edit the button text and the linked level name.

3. Press the play button in the Unity editor to test your scene and ensure that your tutorial button is displaying and functional.

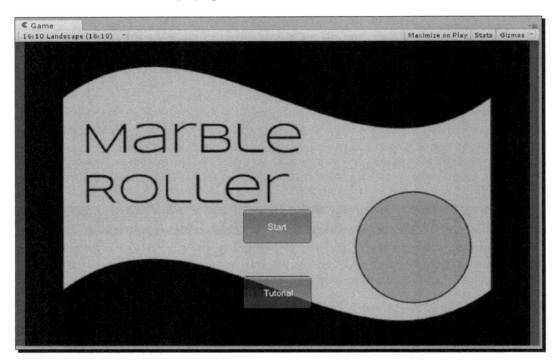

What just happened?

Your tutorial scene was already capable of exiting the menu, but before you created a button to access it, the player had no way to get there in the first place. Now that you can get to the tutorial from the title screen and then back again, the tutorial is fully integrated into the game loop, and it now provides a way for new players to experiment without overwhelming them with challenges right off the bat.

Creating a following camera in Unity

One of the most important features to polish in your project is your camera. Game cameras are just as important as movie cameras because they frame everything the player sees in your game world. They can also feature smooth and intuitive controls that aid with immersion. So far, we've only covered fixed-position cameras that look at our target, but in this section, we'll create a third-person camera that follows our marble as it moves.

Time for action – creating a following third-person camera

A large portion of games use some variant of a following third-person camera, including marble-rolling games like the one we've been using as an example. These cameras typically follow the target around while maintaining a set distance and elevation.

First, we'll need to disable our current camera code, and then we can create a new script for our new camera code. Perform the following steps to create the camera:

1. Click on the **Main Camera** object in the **Hierarchy** window to display its properties in the **Inspector** window.

2. Uncheck the box next to the **Tracking Camera** component to disable it.

    Disabled components are still present on objects, but they don't function as long as the checkbox is empty as shown in the following screenshot:

3. Create a new script called `ThirdPersonCamera.cs` in your `Code` folder, attach it to the **Main Camera** object in the **Hierarchy** window, and open it in your code editor.

The first thing we'll add to the camera is a function that runs for every frame and makes sure the camera is always following the marble.

4. Declare the following variable at the top of the `ThirdPersonCamera` script:

```
public GameObject target;
```

5. Create a new function called `UpdatePosition` in your `ThirdPersonCamera` script and define it as shown in the following code:

```
void UpdatePosition()
{

}
```

6. Add the following lines of code to the function:

```
void UpdatePosition()
{
  //set the camera's position to the target position
  Vector3 targetPosition = target.transform.position;
  transform.position = targetPosition;

  //move the camera away from the target according to an
  //offset value
  Vector3 forwardOffset = transform.forward * -5;
  Vector3 upwardOffset = transform.up * 5;
  transform.Translate(new Vector3(0, upwardOffset.y,
    forwardOffset.z, Space.World);
}
```

Let's examine the previous code, which is divided into two main steps: setting the camera to match the position of the target object and then moving the camera up and away from the target using two offset values.

The first step creates a `Vector3` value to store the position of the target and then accesses the target through the `GameObject` target you declared earlier to retrieve the data. It then sets the camera's current position to the retrieved position as a starting point for the next step, the offset step.

First, we declare a `Vector3` value for the forward offset, which we set to the camera's `transform.forward` property and multiply it by a magnitude of `-5` (the number is negative because we're moving backwards away from the camera). We create an upwards offset in the same way, but we use `transform.up` instead of `transform.forward` so that the offset vector lies along the *y* axis. We then translate the camera by the `Y` value of the upward offset and the `Z` value of the forward offset in world space, leaving the `X` value at zero because we don't require any lateral movement.

When defining relative space in a Translate operation, there are two options: Self and World. The Self space moves the object according to its local axes or the axes bound to the object's current orientation. The World space moves the object according to the global position axes, which means the direction of movement won't be affected by orientation.

As our new function positions the camera at a higher elevation than the marble, using our new positioning function alone leaves the marble out of frame, as shown in the following screenshot:

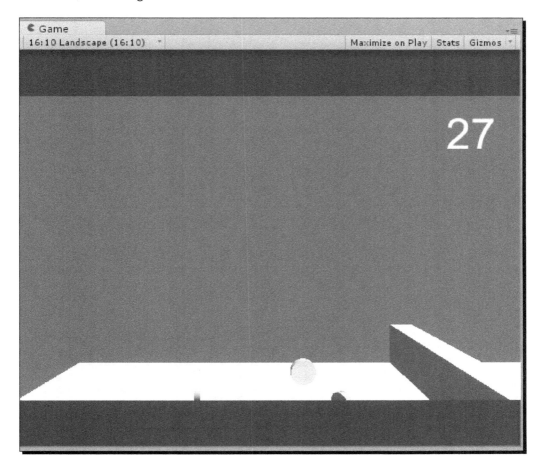

We should create another function that corrects the orientation of the camera so that it keeps the marble in the center of the screen. The easiest way to do this is with the LookAt function.

7. Add an `UpdateRotation` function to your `ThirdPersonCamera` script.

8. Add the following lines to the function:

```
void UpdateRotation()
{
  //rotate the camera to look at our target
  transform.LookAt(target.transform);
}
```

The last step before testing our camera is adding calls to our new functions in the `Update` function.

9. Add the following lines to the `Update` function in the `ThirdPersonCamera` script:

```
void Update()
{
  UpdatePosition();
  UpdateRotation();
}
```

Now we're ready to link the target to our public variable slot and test our camera's new functionality.

10. Set your marble as the target of `ThirdPersonCamera` by clicking-and-dragging it from the **Hierarchy** window to the **Target** field in the **Main Camera** object's **Inspector** window.

11. Press the play button in the Unity editor to test your new camera functions.

The camera should now follow the movement of the marble and keep it in the center of the view from an elevated third-person perspective, as shown in the following screenshot:

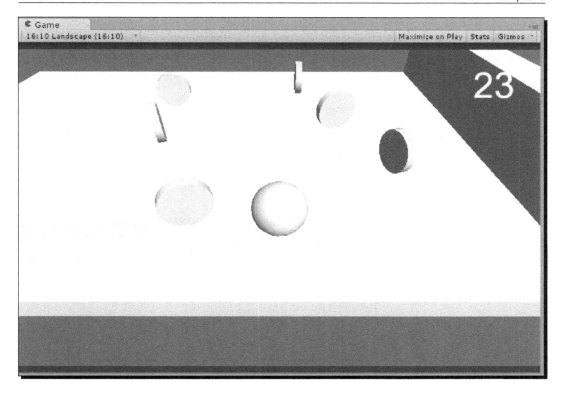

What just happened?

You've successfully implemented a following third-person camera that follows your player around the game world instead of being stationary. Your constantly updating offset means you can make your levels as big as you want without worrying that your marble will leave the camera's view boundaries.

Have a go hero – add rotation controls to your camera

Now that you've explored the camera functionality in a little more depth, you can start to apply that knowledge to build advanced camera scripts that present your game in just the way you want.

For a challenge, try editing your `UpdateRotation` function to enable user rotation control that orbits the camera around the target marble. Use your user knowledge from *Chapter 4, Moving Your Player with Controller Input*, and combine it with your new knowledge of offsets, rotation, and translation (in both `World` space and `Self` space).

Keep in mind that your input is still based on perspective, so the rotation of the camera won't affect the direction of movement. This is disorienting to some players, so if you decide to incorporate a rotating camera, make sure to change your marble's movement code to account for the camera's `transform.forward` vector.

Need a good jumping-off point? Unity's built-in third-person controller is a good place to get some ideas. Import it by clicking on **Assets** on the top toolbar and selecting **Character Controller** from the **Import Package** menu. You can then find the code files in the `Standard Assets` folder in your **Project** window and open them in your code editor to see how they work.

Time for action – adding audio to your game

No game is complete without audio, and fortunately it's relatively simple to integrate in Unity. In this tutorial, we'll demonstrate how to add audio to your Unity project by creating a sound effect that plays whenever a coin is collected. Perform the following steps to add audio:

1. Click on your `Coin` prefab in the **Project** window to display its properties in the **Inspector** window.

2. Click on the **Add Component** button in the **Inspector** window and select **Audio Source** from the **Audio** menu.

   The **Audio Source** component has several properties that can be set in the **Inspector** window, as shown in the following screenshot:

The **Audio Clip** region is where you'll add the sound effect file that you want to play.

The **Play On Awake** checkbox, which is enabled by default, dictates whether the **Audio Source** component plays **Audio Clip** as soon as it's created.

3. We only want the coin's **Audio Clip** to play when it's collected, so uncheck the box next to **Play On Awake**.

Before you add in your first audio clip, it's a good idea to create a dedicated folder for it and other sound effects in your `Assets` directory.

4. Create a new folder in your **Project** window and name it `Audio`.

5. Click-and-drag any Unity-compatible sound effect to the `Audio` folder.

 Any audio file with the extension `.aif`, `.wav`, `.mp3`, or `.ogg` can be used as a sound effect or music track in the Unity engine. If you need to find sound effects, there are several free sound databases, such as `http://www.freesound.org/`, that game developers use for the same purpose.

6. Drag the audio file from your `Audio` folder in your **Project** window to the **Audio Clip** field in the **Inspector** window.

When your audio clip is loaded, you will see its name next to the **Audio Clip** label as well as a gray information box that says **This is a 3D Sound.**, as shown in the following screenshot:

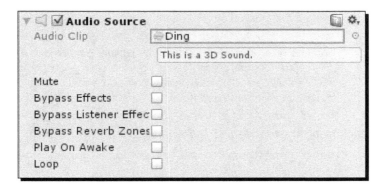

A `3D Sound` in Unity is a sound that has a physical location in the game world. The distance from the player and the player's rotation affects the way the sound is played, enabling them to identify where something is around them or how far away it is.

In the case of our rolling marble game, we want our sound to play when the player picks up a coin, but the location of the sound doesn't matter. Therefore, we'll turn this audio clip into a `2D Sound` by editing its import properties.

7. Click on your audio clip in the **Project** window to display its import settings in the **Inspector** window.

The **3D Sound** checkbox is the second object from the top, as shown in the following screenshot:

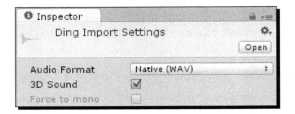

8. Uncheck the box next to **3D Sound** to use your sound effect as a 2D sound.

Audio Source on the Coin prefab is now ready to play your audio file, but we still have to script a trigger for it.

9. Create a new script called CoinSound.cs, attach it to your Coin prefab, and open it in your code editor.

10. Add a function in the script that extends Unity's OnTriggerEnter function as shown in the following code:

```
void OnTriggerEnter(Collider obj)
{

}
```

You may recall that our Coin prefab's collider is marked as a trigger, so collisions are reported through OnTriggerEnter. If the collider wasn't marked as a trigger, you would extend OnCollisionEnter instead.

11. Add the following line to the OnTriggerEnter function as shown:

```
void OnTriggerEnter(Collider obj)
{
   gameObject.GetComponent<AudioSource>().Play();
}
```

In the previous line, we use the GetComponent function on the Coin object to retrieve the audio source we added, and then we triggered it by calling the Play function.

12. Click on the play button in the Unity editor and roll the marble into a coin to hear your new sound effect.

What just happened?

You've now successfully added an **Audio Source** component to an existing prefab and triggered **Audio Clip** to play with a script. Now that you have done this, you can add sound effects and music tracks to anything using the same method. Try having your menu buttons make a click noise, or add a sound effect to your marble that plays whenever the player presses the jump button.

If you're adding music to your game, try using the **Loop** property in the **Audio Source** component window so that the music plays as long as your player is in the game even if the song ends.

Packaging your project for submission

Publishing a piece of art for the entire world to see is intimidating, and games are no exception. Once you're completely satisfied with the feel, aesthetic, and general play style of your game, you're ready to package it for submission to the OUYA marketplace where OUYA players all around the world can download and experience your game.

The last thing you have to do before submitting your game is to create an entry for it on the OUYA developer portal, which will allow you to check the status of your review and publish it when it is accepted. It's also where you will write the description of your game, assign it a content rating, and include any notes to the reviewers that you'd like them to read.

Time for action – creating your game on the developer portal

The first time you create a game on the developer portal, you'll have to set up your account, which includes completing your developer profile and the marketplace agreement. Perform the following steps to create the game:

1. Open a web browser and navigate to the link `https://devs.ouya.tv/developers/games`.

2. Click on **Add a Game**.

The portal will automatically redirect you to a window where you can see what developer information still needs to be completed.

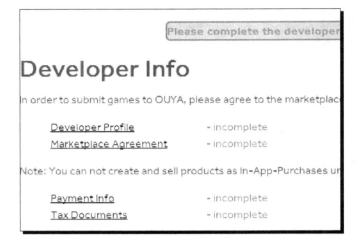

The top two elements, **Developer Profile** and **Marketplace Agreement**, are required for any game to be submitted for publication on the OUYA marketplace. The last two elements, **Payment Info** and **Tax Documents**, are only required if your project contains any sort of sale as an in-app purchase.

3. Open the **Developer Profile** link in a new window and fill out all of the required information on the following page.

4. Click on **Save** and close the window.

5. Refresh the **Developer Info** window and ensure that the **Developer Profile** section is now marked as **Done**.

6. Open the **Marketplace Agreement** link in a new window and read the provided document. Mark the checkbox if you agree to the terms and click on **Agree**.

7. Click on **Save** and close the window.

At this point, you can either continue with the **Developer Info** page and complete the remaining steps that are required for a game with in-app purchases, or if your game is completely free, you can continue to submission.

8. Navigate to the following link:

`https://devs.ouya.tv/developers/games/new`

9. Fill in the required information, review each mandatory checkbox, and double-check to make sure your Android package name matches your bundle ID in your Unity project (something like `com.YourSite.YourGame`).

10. When you're ready, press **Create**. You will be taken to a page where you can enter more information about your game such as a description or input notes for the reviewer.

11. After inserting all the required information, it's now ready for the game's APK file. Whenever the game is final and ready to be published, you can upload it on this page.

That's it! You've taken your OUYA experience to the end of the line. You may not be ready to upload your first game right after finishing this chapter, but as soon as you're ready, return to this chapter and use it as a guide to share your creation with the world.

What just happened?

The OUYA Developer Portal is the final destination for the projects that you're ready to publish and potentially sell. The submission process is subject to change as well as the content guidelines, but the latest steps and requirements will always be available from the Developer Portal site, so make sure that you examine the resources and checklists there before adding games to your My Games list for review. Typically, games take three days to receive a review, but that timeline may change depending on how many submissions they receive in addition to your own. The review process is generally lenient, but the OUYA team will let you know if you need to alter any content before it's allowed on the marketplace.

Pop quiz – the end of the beginning

Q1. Which of the following criteria is not required by the OUYA Content Submission Guidelines?

1. All vital game elements within the "safe zone"
2. Multiplayer functionality
3. No hate speech or derogatory content
4. Game doesn't crash

Q2. Where should you instantiate the `OuyaGameObject` prefab that's necessary for all OUYA games made in Unity?

1. In the final scene
2. In the title screen scene
3. In the game scene
4. In the first scene to be loaded

Q3. If you want to move an object through the game world based on its orientation, which space should you specify in the `Translate` function?

1. `World` space
2. `Self` space
3. `Scene` space
4. `Game` space

Summary

In this chapter, you took an unfinished game prototype, polished it, and prepared it for publishing by making sure it met all of the OUYA submission guidelines. You made sure that all game elements are visible on the screen by containing them within the safe zone.

You also created two unique icons for your game that will distinguish it and serve as a cover for it on the OUYA marketplace and on the OUYA menu.

You also learned how to present your game cleanly with a title screen, end screen, and tutorial screen. You also learned how to use **GUI Texture** objects and **GUI** buttons, which you can combine with your knowledge of **GUI Text** to create any user interface you can imagine. You also learned how to play audio in your games using the **Audio Source** object type.

You've now experienced every facet of game development for the OUYA in Unity, from setting up a project to submitting it for publication.

The next chapter will be focused on ways that you can keep growing and lay a self-sustainable foundation of development knowledge so that if you can think it, you can create it.

9
Blazing Your Own Development Trail

Now that you've learned all the fundamental basics of making games for OUYA, it's time to turn your gaze outward and create a plan that will help you keep learning beyond the content featured in this book. The previous chapter covered the last remaining basics for game development, including polishing mechanics and structure and submitting finished projects to the OUYA marketplace. This chapter will give you a springboard of resources that will teach you how to teach yourself as well as focus on some development methodologies and tricks of the trade used by both indie and professional developers alike.

This chapter will cover the following topics:

◆ Expanding your skills with advanced challenges

◆ Popular game development methodologies

◆ Basic design patterns for large code projects

◆ Getting started with version control

◆ Finding your own answers to questions online

The advanced challenges in the first section of this chapter will offer a starting point and hints on achieving their goals, but there will only be a few strict tutorials; instead, the challenges will serve as puzzles that can be figured out by applying everything you've learned in the previous chapters.

Expanding your skills with advanced challenges

While this book has covered every essential element of an OUYA game, it would be impossible to document all of the complexities and variations there are in each facet of game development. Between graphical effects, camera control, mechanical tweaking, and GUI polishing, there's always a way to make each distinct element of your game better. In this section are several challenges (and a few tutorials) that will challenge your development skills and inspire you to go beyond what you already know.

Working with shaders in depth

We've already done some basic work with shaders in *Chapter 6, Saving Data to Create Longer Games*, which are great tools that allow us to customize the finer aspects of a graphical object, such as how light hits it. However, we only touched upon the `Diffuse` and `Specular` shaders, whereas there are many more complex shaders that can give your game an entirely different feel.

Try exploring the different categories of shaders that are already included in every Unity project. You'll find that there are various standard `Diffuse` and `Specular` shaders for each category, but they all offer different primary functionality.

The following table outlines the default Unity shader categories:

Shader category	Description
FX	FX shaders focus on special effects such as lens flares, which is what the included `Flare` shader does.
GUI	GUI shaders manage on-screen elements that aren't part of your game world. The included `Text Shader` is necessary for all materials that you apply to in-game fonts.
Mobile	The shaders in the `Mobile` category are designed to run efficiently on weaker mobile technology and work around all of the technological differences between desktop and mobile development.
Nature	`Nature` shaders are meant to be applied to the outdoor components of your scene, including grass, trees, and terrain. You're likely to have many repeating nature assets in an outdoor game world, so `Nature` shaders are important for both appearance and efficiency.
Particles	`Particle` shaders can create several different effects when particles overlap, such as making them brighter or multiplying their color values.
Reflective	`Reflective` shaders sample the world around them and accurately reflect other objects in the world like a mirror. `Reflective` shaders are only available in the Pro version of the Unity engine.
RenderFX	`RenderFX` shaders are used to create effects that change how an object is rendered, such as turning a cube into a skybox.

Shader category	Description
Self-Illumin	Self-Illumin shaders are just what they sound like: objects that don't require a light present in the scene to be seen easily.
Sprites	Sprites shaders are used to display the game elements in 2D games that aren't affected by 3D lighting.
Transparent	Transparent shaders allow the user to see through an object to whatever is behind it. Opacity levels can be adjusted with a slider in the **Inspector** window.
Unlit	Unlit shaders don't respond to 3D lighting and have their own uniform shading.

Time for action – creating a custom font with a text shader

You've already displayed text in your prototypes, but up until this point, we've been using the standard Arial font. However, you can display text in any Unity-compatible font using a Text Shader; the steps are as follows:

1. Create a new material and select **Text Shader** from the GUI list in the **Shader** drop-down menu.

A custom material with a Text Shader material attached to it has an area where you can input a texture in the **Inspector** window, as shown in the following screenshot:

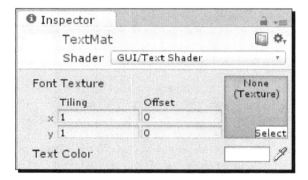

2. Add this texture to your asset list by importing a font file into your project and using the resulting font texture.

3. Next, link the Text Shader material to a GUI Text object and make sure that it is displayed properly on the screen.

If you've configured the material and shader properly, you should be able to change the color of the displayed text in real time by changing the **Text Color** property of the material you created.

The following example shows a `GUI Text` object with a `Text Shader` material on it that features Microsoft's *IMPACT* font:

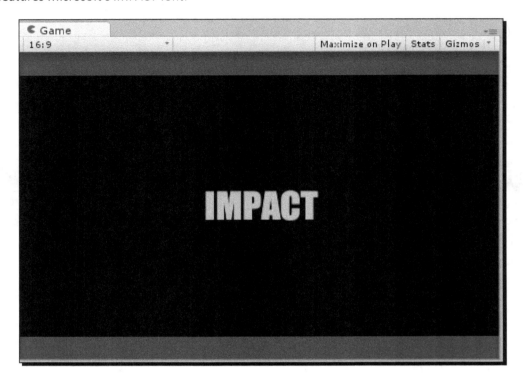

What just happened?

Text shaders let you customize the appearance of your on-screen text, just like how graphical shaders let you customize your mesh objects. Text shaders require a texture that can be acquired through importing any Unity-compatible font into your project.

You just followed this process to create your first custom font. Now that you know how to do it, you can choose fonts that mirror the tone of your game instead of using potentially dull default fonts.

Time for action – creating a fire effect with a particle shader

Basic `Particle System` objects in Unity don't look very distinct; by default, they emit white particles in an inverted cone shape that slowly travel upwards, as shown in the following screenshot:

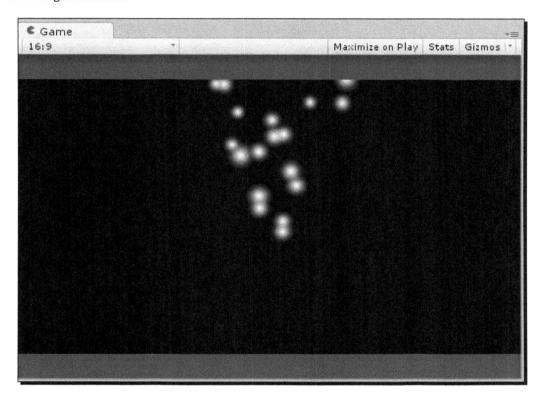

Before you knew about shaders, it was impossible to change the color or graphical effects on any `Particle System` object. However, you now know how to create materials with custom shaders that can be applied to any game object, including `Particle System` objects:

1. Create a `Particle` shader with an `Additive` effect so that the particles look brighter when they overlap.

2. Use this in combination with the `Particle System` properties in the **Inspector** window to create a semi-realistic fire effect, as demonstrated in the following screenshot:

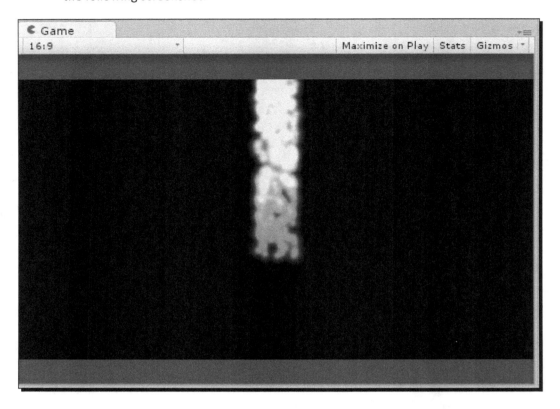

The torch effect in the preceding example makes use of the **Emission**, **Shape**, and **Color over Lifetime** properties of the `Particle System` objects. The more you enable, the more you can customize your effect to look just right.

What just happened?

You've had your first taste of the expansive Shuriken particle system that's integrated into Unity. Every optional component in a particle system's **Inspector** window features a simple user interface to customize different properties of your particles, so you can use Shuriken to create any kind of particle-based effect you want.

Particle shaders also offer different blending types, such as `Multiply` and `Additive`, which change the way they appear when they overlap. Blending types can be used in tandem with the custom particle settings to create any particle-based effect you can imagine.

Try experimenting with the different shaders available to you in the shader list. Note that advanced shader effects such as reflection and render textures can only be used with the Pro version of Unity, but there's still an immense library in the free version to get started with. For more tips and tutorials on customizing your graphics with shaders, a good place to start is Unity's ShaderLab documentation, which can be found at http://docs.unity3d.com/Documentation/Components/SL-Reference.html.

Advanced data saving

In *Chapter 6, Saving Data to Create Longer Games*, you learned how to store data and retrieve it by making the number of coins collected consistent between play sessions using Unity's PlayerPrefs functions. However, saving single numbers is just the tip of the iceberg when it comes to data management in larger projects.

Time for action – saving the player's position

In a game with massive levels, the player may need to quit in the middle of a session. They could get frustrated if their position resets to the initial start zone instead of picking up where they left off; nobody wants to play the same part of the game twice just because they had to stop the first time:

1. Implement a system that saves the player's current location whenever they exit the game and respawns them at their saved location whenever the game is started again.

    You can achieve this in the same way that you saved the number of coins, but keep in mind that the position data is stored as Vector3 and PlayerPrefs doesn't have a SetVector3 function.

    There isn't a single right way to go about saving data that's not natively supported by PlayerPrefs. Instead, it's all about how you want to implement the system and manipulate the data in a way that makes sense.

2. Try saving each individual axis value as a floating-point number or an integer (using SetFloat or SetInt, respectively), and then set the *x*, *y*, and *z* coordinates of the player one by one at the start of the game.

    For minimum data usage, you could convert the entire Vector3 value into a single string value and then parse it on load using the string Split and Trim functions along with the C# Convert class.

 Saving the position data is a good way to store progress in higher levels, but what about games that have several levels? It's simpler than you think. This is because the Application.LoadLevel function can take a string as a parameter to load a level; you can simply save the name of the current scene as a string and use it to load whichever level the player left on.

What just happened?

Being a skilled programmer sometimes comes down to knowing how to manipulate data to make it do what you want, even if it isn't explicitly designed for that purpose. In the previous section, you explored methods to manipulate simple datatypes to represent meaningful data and learned how to parse multiple values from one stored string.

To challenge yourself, try playing a game that features saving/loading functionality and try to figure out how you would save each property of that game. Think of the minimal amount of information needed to store your process and how that would be stored in numbers and letters.

Making a more polished GUI

The GUI is one of the most important elements of any game because it's always on the screen; user interfaces are much like windows through which we see the game world, so it's important to have a clean, unobtrusive window that tells our player what they need to know.

Time for action – creating a reusable GUI Skin

You used a standard GUI button earlier when you created a title screen with a **Start** and **Tutorial** button in *Chapter 8, Polishing and Prepping Your Game for Deployment*. However, you didn't change the default appearance of the buttons, so they appeared as standard transparent gray boxes, as shown in the following screenshot:

These boxes are clean and functional, but if we want them to match the unique theme of our game, we'll have to apply a GUI Skin. Just like every other reusable asset, a GUI Skin can be created and stored in your **Project** window and edited in the **Inspector** window; the steps to do so are as follows:

1. Create a new GUI Skin and edit the various fonts and textures in the GUI Skin **Inspector** window until you've achieved a personalized look for your buttons.

2. When you want to apply a GUI Skin to your current buttons, create a variable of type GUISkin named `marbleGameSkin` in the script that manages your GUI and add the following lines to your OnGUI function:

```
void OnGUI()
{
  GUI.skin = marbleGameSkin;
  //GUI drawing code goes here
}
```

3. Customize and test the skin until everything looks as it should.

When you're finished, your GUI theme should feel flush with the rest of the game, just like the following screenshot:

What just happened?

You've just made Unity's GUI system your own by customizing your buttons to use your own texture. A GUI that matches the tone and aesthetic of your game will always help to satisfy and immerse your player, and you can reuse your custom elements by creating GUI Skin objects like the one you just made.

Time for action – making an automatically scaling GUI texture

The logo of our marble game may fill the screen in the **Game** window, but it may not be big enough to cover the entire view area when it's running on fullscreen on OUYA. Fortunately, there's an easy trick you can apply to make your fullscreen textures automatically scale to the size of your screen, and it doesn't even require any code:

1. In order to have an autoscaling texture, you need to remove all the **Pixel Inset** values from the **Inspector** window of the logo's **GUITexture**. Set the **X**, **Y**, **W**, and **H** values of **Pixel Inset** to 0.

2. Your logo should now have no nonzero values besides the centered **X** and **Y** position values (at **0.5** each) and the **Z** scale (at **1**). This is shown in the following screenshot:

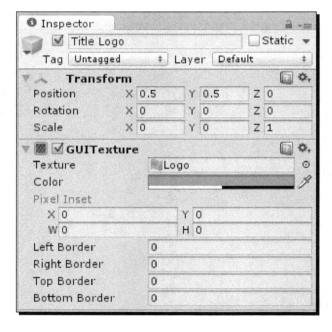

3. With these settings, your logo will disappear from your **Game** window, but we can make it show up again by editing the **X** and **Y** scale values.

4. Change the **X** and **Y** scale values to 1.

Your logo should now perfectly fill the **Game** window, no matter how you size it. The edges of the logo should be touching all four borders of the window, just like the following screenshot:

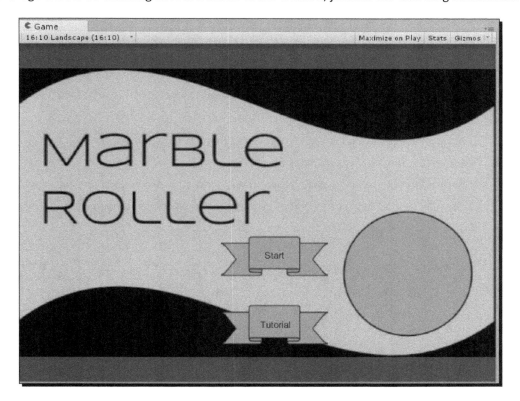

What just happened?

Even though it's slightly counterintuitive, setting all of your logo's **Pixel Inset** values to **0** is the fastest way to center and scale any texture on screen. Keep in mind, however, that there are some downfalls to this method; if you edit the **Border** properties, the logo will tile itself to fill the screen. For instances when you need a border, try setting the width and height of your logo to `Screen.width` and `Screen.height` in a script, respectively.

Lighting your scenes perfectly

A simple scene doesn't take more than a few seconds to light, but if you want to set a mood in your game and create an added sense of realism using lighting, Unity features a few tools that can make your objects catch the light just right and cast high-definition shadows behind them.

Time for action – adding realism to your scene with lightmapping

Lightmapping in Unity is a quick and powerful process that can add detailed shadows and object lighting to make your game world appear even more real. To demonstrate this, we'll create a basic scene with primitive objects and preview it before and after lightmapping:

1. Create a new scene in Unity named `lightmappingDemo`.

2. Create a plane positioned at 0, 0, 0 for our objects to sit on.

3. Create three cubes and position them next to each other on the plane.

4. Give each cube a different material color or size.

5. Create a point light and position it so that it lights the three cubes and the plane.

    Your fully assembled scene should look something like the following screenshot:

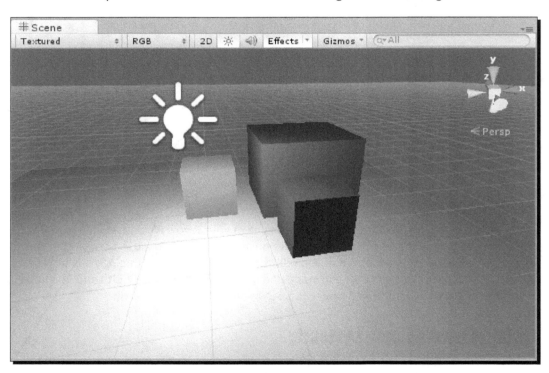

As you can see, none of the cubes have cast shadows yet. Directional lights can project shadows across any kind of object automatically, but point lights require lightmapping to cast shadows.

6. Open the **Window** menu on the topmost toolbar of the Unity editor and select **Lightmapping**.

7. Click on your point light in the **Hierarchy** window to display its **Lightmapping properties** in the **Lightmapping** window.

8. Change the **Baked Shadows** property to **On (Realtime: Soft Shadows)**.

   The other properties of the light can remain at their default values for this example. Your point light settings should look like the following screenshot:

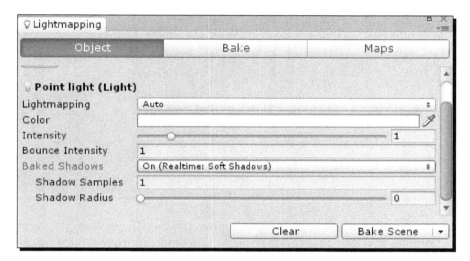

9. Keeping the *Ctrl* key pressed on Windows or *command* key pressed on Mac, click to select all three cubes in your scene's **Hierarchy** window while keeping your point light selected.

10. Once all of your objects are selected, mark the box next to **Lightmap Static** to include all of them in the lightmapping operation.

11. Click on the **Bake Scene** button and wait for the operation to complete.

> **Baking** is the process of analyzing a scene or object with a high level of detail and then saving the data so that it can be used without performing expensive detailed calculations in real time. Lightmaps aren't the only thing that can be baked; 3D artists can create the illusion of extreme detail by calculating lighting information onto their models and baking that lighting information onto a less detailed version of the model.

12. When the scene is lightmapped, change the **Lightmapping** setting to **BakedOnly** to see the effect of your bake.

Your baked scene will look like the following screenshot:

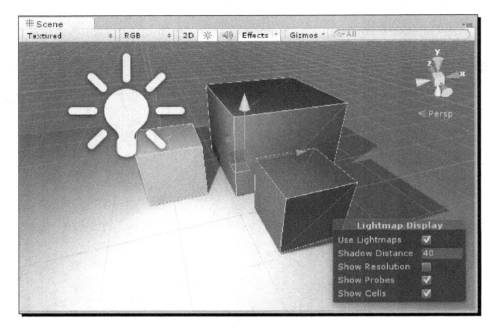

As you can see, each cube now casts its own shadow, and there is some slight coloration on the plane from the light that bounces off the cube. These effects can be modified using the light settings in the **Lightmapping** window, so play around with them until you find one that suits the mood of your scene.

What just happened?

You just added a lightmap to a scene by "baking" lighting detail onto all of your static objects. Adding a lightmap lets your point lights cast shadows, and it also enables you to create several advanced lighting effects, such as light pouring in through a window or bouncing off colored objects.

Have a go hero – experiment with Light Probes in Unity Pro

While lightmapping static objects is possible in any version of Unity, the Pro version enables you to simulate the effect of lightmapping on nonstatic objects, such as your character. This simulation is done using `Light Probes`.

If you have Unity Pro or have activated a free trial for it, open it up and try your hand at creating a scene filled with `Light Probes`. If you're looking for a starting point, explore the Unity documentation page on `Light Probes` at `http://docs.unity3d.com/Documentation/Manual/LightProbes.html`.

Making your world feel real with Physics Materials

Physics Materials are like materials for your object's collider. Instead of affecting the appearance of the object, they affect the way things physically collide with it. For instance, a ball rolling on ice isn't going to behave in the same way as a ball rolling on rubber.

In this section, we'll demonstrate how to apply a Physics Material to an object and then provide a couple of challenges where you can attempt to make a physical/elemental prototype.

Time for action – applying an ice Physics Material

In this tutorial, we'll quickly set up a scene with a tilted platform that we'll attach an ice Physics Material to and see how it affects an object on top of it:

1. Create a new scene in Unity named physicsMaterialDemo.

2. Create a cube, position it at 0, 0, 0, and set its **X** and **Z** scale values to 5.

3. Add a directional light to your scene with the default orientation.

4. Create and apply a transparent blue specular material to give it an "icy" look.

   Your initial scene setup should look something like the following screenshot:

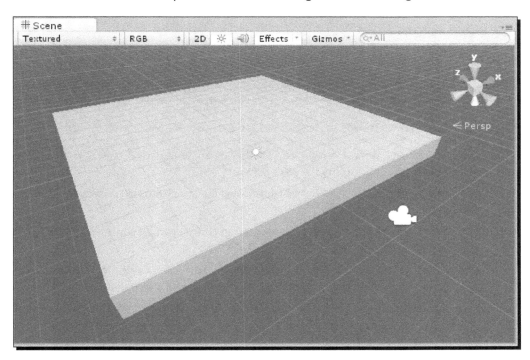

5. Change the **X** rotation of the platform to -20 so that it's tilted towards the camera.

6. Create a primitive cube and place it at the upper-most corner of the tilted platform.

7. Press **Play** to test the scene and watch the cube fall into place on the platform.

Note that the cube doesn't slide because we haven't applied a `Physics Material` yet; it simply stays put.

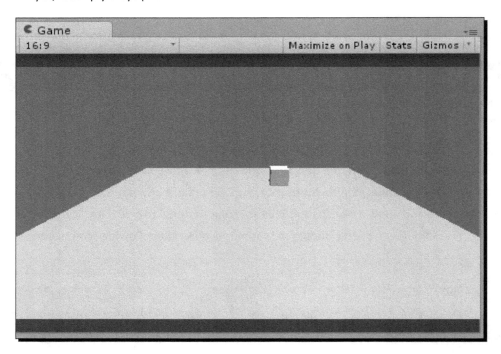

Next, we'll set up the ice material so that we can see how it affects the cube.

8. Open the **Assets** menu from the top toolbar of the Unity editor and select **Physics Materials** under the **Import Package** list.

9. Click on **Import** to add the **Physics Materials** files to a **Standard Assets** folder in your **Project** window.

10. Click on the cube you're using as a platform in the **Hierarchy** window to display it in the **Inspector** window.

11. Click-and-drag the **Ice** material from the **Physics Materials** folder inside **Standard Assets** and drop it in the **Material** field of your platform's **Box Collider** component.

12. Press **Play** again to see the cube fall on the platform with an attached `Physics Material`.

In the following screenshot, observe how the lessened friction on the platform causes the cube to slide downwards towards the camera:

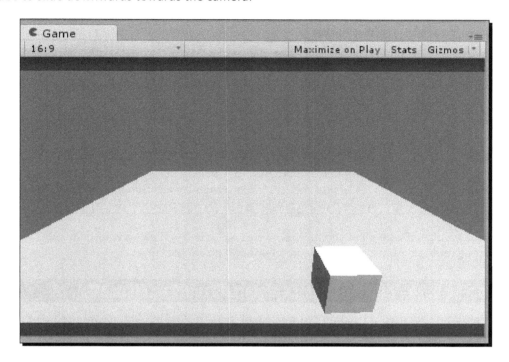

 You don't always have to use the `Physics Materials` offered in the **Standard Assets** folder; you can also create your own by opening the **Assets** menu from the top toolbar of the Unity editor and selecting **Physics Materials** from the **Create** menu.

What just happened?

You've just taken your first step into giving the objects in your game world realistic physical properties. Adding `Physics Materials` is a great way to add some diversity to your game and can even help make core mechanics more fun with unexpected properties (sliding on ice, bouncing on a bouncy surface).

Have a go hero – playing with other Physics Materials

The best way to learn how to effectively use `Physics Materials` is to play with the ones included in Unity. Add each of the `Physics Materials` from the **Standard Assets** folder to your tilted platform and see how they affect your cube.

The following table provides a brief description of each of the five standard `Physics Materials`:

Physics Material	Description
Bouncy	This material makes objects that hit it bounce back with a force relative to their impact.
Ice	This material drastically reduces friction on objects, causing them to lose grip and slide.
Metal	Metal is slick, but not as much as ice, and objects don't pick up speed on them quite as fast.
Rubber	Rubber surfaces provide the ultimate grip, reducing momentum and keeping the friction at a maximum.
Wood	The wood material's friction values are almost exactly halfway between ice and rubber, providing a happy middle ground for typical objects.

Once you've played with all of the `Physics Materials`, try making your own and combining multiple materials to make an elemental obstacle course.

Have a go hero – making Physics Materials react realistically

Wouldn't it be cool if your ice didn't just cause objects to slide but actually melted and disappeared when exposed to fire? This type of functionality isn't built into `Physics Materials`, but you certainly know enough at this point to script some cool extra effects. Here are a few ideas to implement in your `Physics Material` demo:

◆ An ice object that destroys itself when it collides with a fire particle

◆ A fire particle system that gets bigger the more wood it touches

◆ A "boing" sound effect that plays whenever something hits a bouncy object

Make sure to experiment with colliders on the `Particle System` objects to implement any effects that involve fire or other particle-based objects.

Popular game development methodologies

Planning and organizing your project can be as much of an art as actually developing it. In this section, you'll learn a few different methodologies that you can follow to ensure that your game follows a logical development pattern suited for you or your team.

The Waterfall model

One of the most popular and oldest development patterns is the **Waterfall model**, dating back to 1970. The Waterfall model takes its name from its cascading stages of development, with each stage flowing into the next until the final stage is reached. These stages are outlined in a basic Waterfall model as follows:

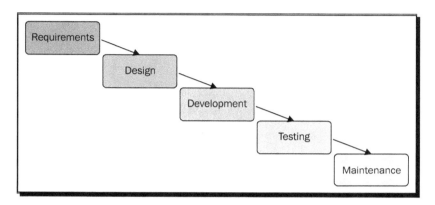

The Waterfall model has been lauded and criticized alike for its idealistic nature. Some developers argue that it's irresponsible to begin the next stage of a project before finishing the current one because a lot of early planning can be more advantageous than on-the-fly development. Others believe that every stage of a project is interconnected, and that they should all be developed simultaneously on an iterative basis so that they evolve together and form a cohesive whole.

The latter principle regarding iterative development is exactly what contributed to the inception of the next group of methodologies we'll cover: **Agile development**.

The Agile methodology

Agile is less of a singular methodology and more of a category of methodologies. Agile relies on short incremental cycles instead of a sequential path of development like Waterfall, and in order for Agile to work, the team must communicate efficiently and be open-minded to change. Agile is probably the most common methodology used by modern software developers and is considered to be a great standard for most projects.

Agile was defined in 2001 with a document called the **Agile Manifesto**, which outlined the principles behind the techniques and the necessity of a new system. The Agile Manifesto follows the following twelve principles:

♦   Valuable software should be delivered continuously

♦   Welcome changing requirements regardless of developmental stage

- Deliver working software in a minimal time frame
- Communication between business people and developers is a must
- Reliable team members are motivated and supported
- The best way to share information is face to face
- Working software is the primary measure of progress
- Teams should maintain an intended pace across development cycles
- Good long-term design makes short-term goals easier to achieve
- Simplicity is essential
- Self-organizing teams create better products
- Reflection leads to improvement

 The preceding points are summaries of the twelve guiding principles of the Agile Manifesto. For the full text of the principles as well as the rest of the manifesto, check the page at http://www.agilemanifesto.org.

Most Agile methodologies involve a set time frame for iterations. For instance, a team could set their iteration length to a week or a month, work on a certain element of the project for that length of time, and then revisit it to reflect on what went well and what didn't.

Scrum, arguably the most popular development methodology, strongly promotes Agile development practices. Scrum also adds more definition to the development cycle, thereby creating a more rigid progression for teams so that they function as efficiently as possible. We'll look at the inner workings of a Scrum team next.

The Scrum methodology

Scrum is an Agile development methodology that revolves around the idea of sprints or set increments of time during which the team will iterate on ideas and produce an updated version of their project. Scrum also relies heavily on team roles, which will be reviewed later.

Sprints in Scrum typically last around one to two weeks and require the product to be testable at the end of each sprint so that the next sprint can be planned. Based on the analysis performed after each sprint, a feature is either deemed complete and removed from the project backlog or added into the next sprint to be continued.

A **backlog** is a list of potential features or capabilities that developers can integrate into their game. Backlog entries sometimes come in the form of user stories which present a feature or mechanic from the perspective of the player. For example, a user's story for a new control mechanism may sound something like, "As a user, I want to be able to rotate the camera with the right joystick so that I can easily see my surroundings."

The basic flow of a feature during Scrum development looks like this:

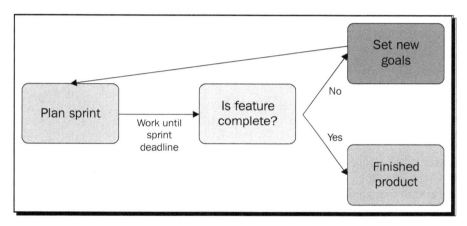

There are three defined roles in the Scrum model: the Product Owner, the Scrum Master, and the Development Team. In this section, we'll dissect each individual role to get a sense of where the responsibilities lie on any given Scrum project:

- **The Product Owner**: The Product Owner represents what your team is striving to create. They are responsible for prioritizing tasks and features, making sure the project stays in scope, and constantly ensuring the value of your final product. The Product Owner can be anyone on your team who has a confident vision of the project and its timeline, but Scrum practices suggest that the Product Owner is not the same as the Scrum Master; we'll look at the alternative duties of the Scrum Master next.

- **The Scrum Master**: The Scrum Master's sole purpose is to uphold the strict development pattern, that is, Scrum. This means organizing and/or conducting sprint meetings and making sure each week's goals are met. The Scrum Master also serves as a conduit between the project leads (including the Product Owner) and the Development Team, which we'll elaborate on next.

◆ **The Development Team**: The Development Team is the group of people responsible for actually creating the game or product. Each Development Team must integrate each sprint goal into a test-friendly environment at the end of a sprint so that the entire project team can make an iterative analysis and decide whether that element is complete or needs another sprint of iteration.

Basic design patterns for larger code projects

Even though our prototypes contain just a handful of scripts, your games will realistically contain many different scripts that will need to interact with each other. Unity's tag system is a great way to create cross-object communication quickly, but for a more reliable and organized approach, there are several design patterns that you can follow to keep your game functional and dynamic. In this section, we'll briefly touch upon the driving philosophies and functions behind three main design patterns and offer implementation ideas to try each of them out in your game.

The Singleton pattern

The Singleton pattern relies on an object with exactly one instance that can usually be accessed from anywhere. The Singleton implementation is equally easy, powerful, and dangerous, and is usually executed with a self-creating accessor function like the following one:

```
public static Singleton getInstance()
{
  if(instance == null)
  {
    instance = CreateInstance();
  }

  return instance;
}
```

The preceding function returns an instance of a singleton that can be accessed without a reference to any object because of the `static` parameter (which is also what guarantees only one instance of the public static variable named `instance`).

You've already had some experience with certain singleton properties, even if you didn't realize it; Unity's tag system essentially makes any object potentially accessible from anywhere using the `GameObject.FindGameObjectsWithTag` function.

So, what's the problem with being able to conveniently access a script's properties from any other script? One or two singletons can improve the efficiency and readability of your code if every system needs to retrieve common data (such as player statistics), but excessive use of singletons can offer a confusing amount of available options during any given situation.

Using singletons to a large extent can also detract from the perceptible architecture of the game, which makes collaborating on your code base with other developers much slower. In summation, singletons are good to use with universal systems, but only use them when you need them; their ease of implementation can lead you into a code design pitfall that's very difficult to escape.

The Factory pattern

The main goal of the Factory pattern is to create several instances of complex objects while keeping the complicated instantiation code hidden from the programmer and avoiding senseless repetition. This can make your code easier to read and can also improve the usability of your code base to new programmers on your project.

Implementation complexity varies because of the myriad of different applications of the Factory pattern. However, a very basic example of a Factory implementation is shown in the following code snippet:

```
GameObject CreateComplexObject()
{
  GameObject newObject = Instantiate(prefab);
  newObject.AddComponent<BoxCollider>();
  newObject.renderer.material.color = Color.red;
  return newObject;
}
```

The `CreateComplexObject` function creates an instance of an existing prefab, adds a box collider to it, and colors it red. If we didn't use it, every place in the script where we wanted to instantiate a collision-ready red object would require all three lines to be written. However, because we encapsulated those three lines into a singular function that returns the premodified object, we can produce this result as many times as we want by calling `CreateComplexObject` in a single line.

The Command pattern

We don't often think about the technology behind the undo/redo commands, but the Command pattern is at the heart of sequential functionality. Implementing this pattern involves encapsulating a single user command or action into its own data type so that it can be stored and repeated at a later time. One such action data type for undoing and redoing a key entry might look like this:

```
class Command
{
  public KeyCode pressedKey;
```

```
   public void Undo()
   {
     //remove the character that matches pressedKey
   }

   public void Redo()
   {
     //add an additional character that matches pressedKey
   }
}
```

A new instance of the `Command` class should be created every time the command is performed and stored in an ever-expanding list of commands so that the user can undo and redo any action and repeat the timeline of events in the same or reverse order. Note that commands shouldn't delete themselves if they are undone because the user may still want to redo them in the future.

Have a go hero – implement one of the preceding patterns

The preceding examples should have given you a good idea of the purpose and general functionality behind different code patterns, but none of the code samples are ready to be pasted into a game just yet; each one is missing a game function, and thus lacking a way to actualize the code.

Come up with a game mechanic that uses one of the three common patterns and implement it in a new or existing Unity project. You won't be able to create a fully fledged implementation of any pattern based on the code samples in this book alone; instead, examine the technical diagrams and descriptions for each pattern on www.oodesign.com before laying out the framework of your new classes and functions. The following are the websites you can refer to:

- The Singleton pattern: http://www.oodesign.com/singleton-pattern.html
- The Factory pattern: http://www.oodesign.com/factory-pattern.html
- The Command pattern: http://www.oodesign.com/command-pattern.html

Getting started with version control

Individual projects are easy to manage, but when multiple people are contributing code to the same project, things can get tricky fast. For instance, imagine keeping the project updated on everyone's computer and sending the project files to everyone every time someone makes a change; it would be inefficient to say the least.

To combat these problems, we can use version control, which is a tool that lets you host your code base on a universal repository and make changes that get pushed to everyone's copy of the project at the same time. Many different version control solutions exist, including Git, SVN, and Perforce; in this section, we'll show you how to set up a private Git repository using a website called BitBucket.

Version control is a complex subject, and we won't be able to cover every aspect of it in this chapter, but Atlassian, the creators of BitBucket, have a great collection of beginner tutorials on their website: `https://www.atlassian.com/git/tutorial`.

Time for action – creating a BitBucket repository

BitBucket is a free website that offers unlimited free private repositories for you and up to four other team members (five members in total). However, before you actually create your repository on the website, you need to create an account. The steps to do so are as follows:

1. Open a web browser and navigate to `https://bitbucket.org`.

2. Click on the button that reads **Sign up for free** and fill in the requested information to create your account.

3. Once you've finished creating your account and have logged in, press the **Create** button at the top of the browser window to create a new repository.

   The **Create a new repository** screen asks for initial information about your project, both optional and required, as shown in the following screenshot:

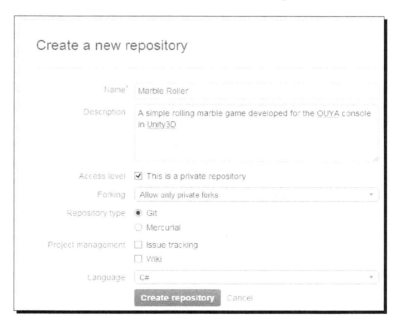

4. Give your repository a name. This is required for all new repositories.

5. If you already know what code you're going to add to the repository, add a simple description in the field labeled **Description**.

6. Keep the checkbox labeled **This is a private repository** selected. Open source projects are public and can be viewed by anyone, but at this point, you probably only want people you've explicitly invited accessing your code.

7. Ensure that your repository type is marked as **Git** and not **Mercurial**.

8. The two checkboxes next to **Project management** are optional, and they offer additional tools to manage a team. Check them if you expect to be working with multiple people on a relatively complex project.

9. Lastly, in the **Language** drop-down menu, select **C#**, as it's the programming language we've been using in Unity.

10. Click on the **Create repository** button. You'll then be taken to the splash screen for a new repository, which offers several steps and suggestions on getting started.

11. Click on the link to **Set up Git** and follow the included instructions to open the Git command line on your computer.

12. Use the following commands to create a new directory for your project files and mark the directory as the origin of your new Git repository:

```
mkdir ~/Projects/MarbleRoller
cd ~/Projects/MarbleRoller
git init
git remote add origin
  https://Username@bitbucket.org/Username/marble-
  roller.git
```

Let's examine the preceding code line by line and see exactly what it's doing.

The `mkdir` command creates a new directory with the path that you specify. If you don't use an absolute path beginning with the drive letter (C:) like in the preceding code example, it begins the path in the directory that the Git command line is currently in.

If you want to change Git's current directory, you can use the second command, `cd`, which stands for "change directory". In the preceding code sample, the `cd` command is used to navigate to the directory that the `mkdir` command created so that Git can explore the root of your project folder.

As soon as the Git command line is looking at your target directory, you can call `git init`, which tells Git to initialize a repository in that directory. The command directly following it, `git remote add origin`, links your initialized Git directory to your repository housed on BitBucket.

 The URL of your Git repository is dependent on your repository name and your username, so the sample code doesn't accurately reflect the location of your new repository. To get the proper URL to use with `git remote add origin`, copy it from the information box next to the **Get started** tab on the new repository screen.

That's it! We'll take care of the other steps on the new repository screen next, but we'll do them on our own, so feel free to navigate back to the BitBucket home page where you can now find your new repository on the right-hand side of the window.

What just happened?

You just created an account on BitBucket and created your first repository, which will in turn give you advanced control over your code base and allow you to invite other users to your repository and contribute their own additions to the project.

Version control requires you to *commit* and *push* any intended changes to your version of the code so that it can be applied to everyone else's copy of the project. In the next tutorial, we'll show you how to add and update files in your repository using these two operations.

Time for action – preparing Unity for version control

Although Git handles text-heavy projects easily, it runs into some trouble when it comes down to binary files, which Unity uses by default to collect and save information about your project. There are, however, a few safety measures that can be put in place to ensure that your project doesn't encounter any errors or bugs when being managed with version control. We'll be demonstrating these measures using our marble game as a reference:

1. Open your `RollingMarble` project in the Unity editor.

2. Open the **Edit** menu on the toolbar at the top of the Unity editor window and select **Editor** within the **Project Settings** submenu.

The **Editor Settings** window will appear in your **Inspector** window and will look something like the following screenshot:

3. If you're using the Pro version of Unity, change your **Asset Serialization** setting to **Force Text**.

If you're using the free version of the Unity software, you'll be unable to edit your **Asset Serialization** setting. This doesn't mean you can't use version control with your Unity project, it just means that you may have to merge files that Git can't automatically merge. For information on manual merges, read the chapter on branching and merging in the Git documentation at `http://git-scm.com/book/en/Git-Branching-Basic-Branching-and-Merging`.

There's one other step to optimizing your Unity project for version control that can be done on any version of Unity: adding a `.gitignore` file. The `.gitignore` file includes names of directories and files that don't need to be shared on the repository, such as the `Library` folder that only stores local build data.

4. Create a new file in your preferred text editor and name it `.gitignore`. Ensure that your text editor doesn't automatically insert an additional extension, such as `.txt`.

5. Add the following lines to the `.gitignore` file:

```
.DS_Store
Library
Temp
*.csproj
*.pidb
*.unityproj
*.sln
*.userprefs
```

In addition to excluding the unnecessary library files, the preceding lines remove files that aren't required to open Unity projects and can create merge errors if left unattended.

6. Save your `.gitignore` file, close it, and move it to the root of your project's directory to be added with your other project files.

> The root directory of your project is the directory that contains folders such as `Assets`, `Library`, `obj`, and `ProjectSettings`. It's important to place your `.gitignore` file in the root of your directory because that's the only place Git will look for it, and if it's in any other folder, the paths in the `.gitignore` file will not be ignored by your repository.

What just happened?

Version control is an invaluable tool to game developers, but that doesn't necessarily mean that every game engine is prepared for version control integration right out of the box.

Unity offers the ability to force text serialization to Pro users, which turns all of the data in your project into characters that Git can automatically merge together.

Users who don't use Unity Pro can still take measures to avoid Git headaches; however, the `.gitignore` files can be used to exclude unnecessary files from your repository while still keeping them present and functioning in their local directory on your own computer.

Time for action – making your first commit and push

Now that you're signed up for BitBucket, you've got an empty repository just waiting for some code. We'll use our marble game files to demonstrate how to upload a project; the steps to do so are as follows:

1. Click-and-drag the entire project directory from its original location to the directory you created for your repository.

2. Open the Git command line and use the `cd` command to navigate to your repository's directory.

As it's the first time we're uploading our project to the repository, we'll want to add every single file with Git. Fortunately, there's a command for that.

3. Enter the following command in your Git command line to add all the files:

```
git add --all
```

This will add changes to all the tracked and untracked files. In the case of projects being added to a repository for the first time, all files are considered to be untracked.

 A tracked file means a file that has already been recognized by Git as part of the working repository, while an untracked file is a file that's been created since your last repository update. In an instance where you want to commit changes to existing code files but erase new temporary ones, you could add each desired change with the `git add filename` command and then discard the rest with the `git checkout -- filename` command.

Your files are now added to the stage to be committed, but until they're committed and pushed, you won't be able to view or access them on your repository—only in your local directory.

4. Enter the following command to commit all the added files:

```
git commit -m "Adding project to repository."
```

The `-a` flag following the commit command tells Git to commit all the added files, and the `-m` flag denotes a commit message. Every commit is required to have a commit message, so don't forget to type a meaningful summary of your changes so that team members can understand the details of the commit at a glance.

The final step, which is taken before your files are uploaded, is to push them to the repository with Git.

5. Enter the following command to push all the committed files:

```
git push origin
```

Using the `push` command updates the repository files with the newer versions that you committed, thereby finalizing the change and enabling other repository members to update their code by using the `git pull` command from the Git command line when they are in their own repository directory.

What just happened?

Even when you save files on your computer while working on your project, these changes won't be reflected on the repository until you add them using the Git command line. The `add`, `commit`, and `push` commands allow us to keep our project repository up to date, while the `pull` command allows us and our fellow team members to ensure they have the latest pushed code before they make changes of their own.

Finding your own answers to questions online

One of the great facts about game development is that if you have a problem, it's likely that someone else has run into the same problem before. A little searching on Google can go a long way, and so can these resources that are specifically tailored to make your development progress smoother and even offer new ideas.

Stack Overflow

Stack Overflow is one of the largest technical question and answer resources on the Internet, not just for Unity and OUYA development, but for all kinds of technical advice and software solutions. Stack Overflow's interface allows correct or smart answers to questions to be voted up and displayed as official answers, so you won't have to scour a results page for the correct solution; often, the answer is right next to the question.

Stack Overflow also rewards users who answer questions with points and medals, so you can use it as an educational resource until you earn enough clout to start educating other users yourself. Start asking and answering at `http://stackoverflow.com`.

OUYA Forums

Remember when we downloaded the OUYA input library from the OUYA Developer Forums in *Chapter 4*, *Moving Your Player with Controller Input*, because it provided a method of processing input that was easier and faster than the standard included input framework? That's just a single example of the myriad of ways in which the OUYA community helps itself grow. New topics are added to the OUYA forums every day, and communicating with your fellow developers is one of the fastest ways to grow. Share ideas, ask questions, and give answers; you have something in common with every OUYA developer, but everyone's experiences are different and can contain valuable lessons about the game industry and creative process in general. The OUYA Developer Forums can be found at `http://forums.ouya.tv`.

Unity Forums

Much like the OUYA Forums, the Unity Forums are a populous thinktank that can provide answers to any questions that have to do with the Unity engine and not things that necessarily apply to OUYA. All of your questions about GameObjects, tags, scripts, and lighting can be found at `http://forum.unity3d.com`.

Pop quiz – leaving the nest

Q1. Which of the following kinds of lights can cast shadows without a lightmap?

1. Area lights
2. Point lights
3. Directional lights
4. Spot lights

Q2. Which of the following design patterns can be used to create complex objects with simple functions?

1. The Singleton pattern
2. The Factory pattern
3. The Command pattern

Q3. Which of the following design patterns can be used to undo and redo a list of actions performed by the user?

1. The Singleton pattern
2. The Factory pattern
3. The Command pattern

Q4. What order should you execute the three basic Git commands in?

1. Commit, add, push
2. Add, commit, push
3. Commit, push, add
4. Push, commit, add

Q5. Which development methodology divides development into sequential stages?

1. Scrum
2. Agile
3. Waterfall
4. Git

Summary

In this chapter, you had the chance to attempt several tutorials that touched on advanced topics that you'll be working with a lot as you make complex games.

You also learned about development methodologies to manage a project from start to finish and how to use version control technologies, such as Git, with services, such as BitBucket, to create and collaborate on small team projects. You also learned how to seek answers for yourself and solve problems pragmatically.

You've reached the end of the book, and you now have the knowledge and resources you need to blaze your own trail without any more basic tutorials. Nobody can learn everything there is about game development, so the more you explore, share, and experiment, the better you'll become. Now go create OUYA games and be a part of the revolution!

Pop Quiz Answers

Chapter 2, Installing Unity and the OUYA ODK

Pop quiz – small parts of a whole

Q1.	3
Q2.	2

Chapter 3, Diving into Development

Pop quiz – hello world

Q1.	2
Q2.	1
Q3.	2

Chapter 4, Moving Your Player with Controller Input

Pop quiz – coming full circle

Q1.	1
Q2.	2

Chapter 5, Enhancing Your Game with Touch Dynamics

Pop quiz – touching the sky

Q1.	1
Q2.	2
Q3.	3

Chapter 6, Saving Data to Create Longer Games

Pop quiz – saving (and loading) the day

Q1.	2
Q2.	2
Q3.	1
Q4.	3
Q5.	2

Chapter 7, Expanding Your Gameplay with In-app Purchases

Pop quiz – talking shop

Q1.	1
Q2.	2
Q3.	3

Chapter 8, Polishing and Prepping Your Game for Deployment

Pop quiz – the end of the beginning

Q1.	2
Q2.	4
Q3.	2

Chapter 9, Blazing Your Own Development Trail

Pop quiz – leaving the nest

Q1.	2
Q2.	2
Q3.	1
Q4.	3
Q5.	2

Index

GUI scripting guide
URL 185
GUI shader 208
GUI Text object
about 177, 184
setting up 128-130
GUI texture
automatically scaling GUI texture,
creating 216, 217
GUI Texture object 182

H

HideCursor function 108
**High-Definition Multimedia Interface
(HDMI) 174**
high scores
in new scene, checking 133-135
reset button, adding to list 138
values, displaying 136, 137

I

Ice material 224
ice Physics Material
applying 221, 222
icons
creating, for game 179
Impulse 94
impulse force
adding, to rigidbody 93, 94
in-app purchases
about 142, 143
consumables 143, 144
entitlements 143
first purchase function, creating 153-156
game, preparing for 144-147
monetization model, picking 168, 169
pricing 167, 168
product, setting up on OUYA developer
portal 144
purchase screen, creating 148-152
successful purchases, loading 157-159
successful purchases, saving 157-159
unlocked functionality, reflecting 160-163
inheritance keyword 40
input library
using 68-70

installation
game engine 15
Unity 16
Instantiate function 93
interactive button
creating 86-92
interactive marble prototype
creating 61
input library, using 68-70
movement control, with OUYA SDK 71-73
scene, setting 62-67
Unity input script, importing 67, 68
Internet settings
configuring 8
isSwiping 102

J

Java
downloading 18, 19
Java Development Kit (JDK) 18
Java JDK package 30
Java Runtime Engine (JRE) 18
JavaShowCursor function 108

K

keyboard interaction
adding, to scripts 52-56

L

lightmapping
used, for adding realism to scene 218-220
Light Probes
URL 220
LookAt function 197
loss screen
creating 186-189

M

Mac OS
PATH variable, editing on 20, 21
Marble object 191
materials 118
Metal material 224
mkdir command 232

mobile shader 208
MonoBehavior keyword 40
mouse position
  reading 96-98
movement control
  with OUYA SDK 71-73
MoveObject function 48
moveVector variable 68, 72
multiple frames
  touch input capturing over 106

N

nature shader 208

O

ObjectMover script 45
Object-oriented programming (OOP) 47
ODK
  downloading 18, 19
OnCollisionEnter function 78, 79
OnGUI function 87, 215
OnTriggerEnter function 121-202
OUYA
  about 7
  first game, installing 9-11
  first test, running 58
  playing 11, 12
OUYA API
  data, saving with 138, 139
OUYA content guidelines 174
OUYA controller
  touch controls 12
OUYA Development Kit 19
OUYA Forums 237
OuyaInput controller framework
  URL 67
OUYA ODK
  movement control, using with 71-73
Ouya ODK package 31
OUYA packages
  exporting from Unity 27, 28
OuyaPurchaseOnSuccess function 156
OUYA touchpad cursor 92
Overscan 174
own camera
  creating 76

P

packages
  Android NDK 31
  Android SDK 30
  importing, into new workspace 28-30
  installing 18-20
  installing, with Android SDK 23
  Java JDK 30
  Ouya ODK 31
particle shader
  fire effect, creating with 211-213
particles shader 208
Particle System object 211
PATH variable
  editing, on Mac OS 20, 21
  editing, on Windows 22
  modifying 20
paygate model 168
Physics Materials
  creating 224
  playing with 223, 224
Pixel Inset property 183
PlayerPrefs
  data, saving with 126, 127
players position
  saving 213
PLAY NOW button 10
Point Light 36
prefab 65
print function 56
product
  setting up, on OUYA developer portal 144
Product Owner, Scrum 227
project
  packaging, for submission 203
public keyword 40

R

reflective shader 208
RenderFX shader 208
reset button
  adding, to high score list 138
reusable GUI Skin
  creating 214-216
rigidbody
  impulse force, adding 93-95

Rotate tool 63
rotation controls
  adding, to camera 199, 200
Rubber material 224

S

save data
  using, in multiple scenes 131
Scale tool 63
scene
  lighting 217
  manipulating 34-36
  realism adding, with lightmapping 218-220
  setting 62-67
Scene window 17
scripts
  keyboard interaction, adding 52-56
  on other objects, accessing 124, 125
Scrum
  about 226, 227
  Development Team 228
  Product Owner 227
  Scrum Master 227
Scrum Master 227
Self-Illumin shader 209
Self space 197
ShaderLab documentation
  URL 213
shaders
  about 208
  FX shader 208
  GUI shader 208
  mobile shader 208
  nature shader 208
  particles shader 208
  reflective shader 208
  RenderFX shader 208
  Self-Illumin shader 209
  sprites shader 209
  Transparent shader 209
  Unlit shader 209
Singleton pattern
  about 228, 229
  URL 230
speed variable 68
Spotlight 36

sprites shader 209
Stack Overflow 237
Start function 40, 41, 75, 137
static functions 132

T

target
  creating, for cannon 109-111
Text Color property 209
text shader
  custom font, creating with 209, 210
Text Shader material 209
ThirdPersonCamera script 198
title screen
  creating 181-185
touch controls 12
touch data
  incorporating, into machines 107
touch input
  capturing, over multiple frames 106
touchpad
  using, to interact with buttons 82
transform.forward property 196
transform.forward vector 200
transform property 120
Translate function 49
Translate tool 63
Transparent shader 209
tutorial
  linking, to game 193, 194
  scene, creating 189-193
typecasting 93

U

Unity
  mouse position, reading 96-98
  OUYA packages, exporting from 27, 28
  preparing, for version control 233-235
  setting up 16, 17
Unity Asset Store packages
  polish, adding with 163-166
Unity engine
  data, saving with 126
Unity Forums 238
Unity input script
  importing 67, 68

Thank you for buying
OUYA Game Development by Example
Beginner's Guide

About Packt Publishing

Packt, pronounced 'packed', published its first book "Mastering phpMyAdmin for Effective MySQL Management" in April 2004 and subsequently continued to specialize in publishing highly focused books on specific technologies and solutions.

Our books and publications share the experiences of your fellow IT professionals in adapting and customizing today's systems, applications, and frameworks. Our solution-based books give you the knowledge and power to customize the software and technologies you're using to get the job done. Packt books are more specific and less general than the IT books you have seen in the past. Our unique business model allows us to bring you more focused information, giving you more of what you need to know, and less of what you don't.

Packt is a modern, yet unique publishing company, which focuses on producing quality, cutting-edge books for communities of developers, administrators, and newbies alike. For more information, please visit our website: www.PacktPub.com.

Writing for Packt

We welcome all inquiries from people who are interested in authoring. Book proposals should be sent to author@packtpub.com. If your book idea is still at an early stage and you would like to discuss it first before writing a formal book proposal, contact us; one of our commissioning editors will get in touch with you.

We're not just looking for published authors; if you have strong technical skills but no writing experience, our experienced editors can help you develop a writing career, or simply get some additional reward for your expertise.

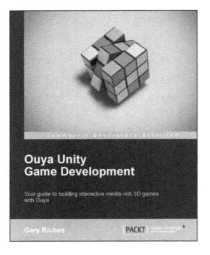

Ouya Unity Game Development

ISBN: 978-1-78355-970-1   Paperback: 118 pages

Your guide to building interactive media-rich 3D games with Ouya

1. Learn how to create and polish your game, and then monetize it with in-app purchases.

2. Discover what's required to make your game run on Android phones and tablets.

3. A step-by-step guide that will teach you how to build a fun, challenging game from scratch.

Unity 4.x Game Development by Example Beginner's Guide

ISBN: 978-1-84969-526-8   Paperback: 572 pages

A seat-of-your-pants manual for building fun, groovy little games quickly with Unity 4.x

1. Learn the basics of the Unity 3D game engine by building five small, functional game projects.

2. Explore simplification and iteration techniques that will make you more successful as a game developer.

3. Take Unity for a spin with a refreshingly humorous approach to technical manuals.

Please check **www.PacktPub.com** for information on our titles

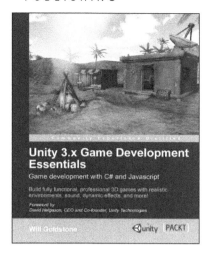

Unity 3.x Game Development Essentials

ISBN: 978-1-84969-144-4   Paperback: 488 pages

Build fully functional, professional 3D games with realistic environments, sound, dynamic effects, and more!

1. Kick start your game development, and build ready-to-play 3D games with ease.

2. Understand key concepts in game design including scripting, physics, instantiation, particle effects, and more.

3. Test & optimize your game to perfection with essential tips-and-tricks.

4. Learn game development in Unity version 3 and above, and learn scripting in either C# or JavaScript.

iOS 7 Game Development

ISBN: 978-1-78355-157-6   Paperback: 120 pages

Develop powerful, engaging games with ready-to-use utilities from Sprite Kit

1. Pen your own endless runner game using Apple's new Sprite Kit framework.

2. Enhance your user experience with easy-to-use animations and particle effects using Xcode 5.

3. Utilize particle systems and create custom particle effects.

Please check **www.PacktPub.com** for information on our titles